Cambridge Elements

Elements in Phonology
edited by
Robert Kennedy
University of California, Santa Barbara
Patrycja Strycharczuk
University of Manchester

PHONOLOGY IN LANGUAGE DOCUMENTATION

Gabriela Caballero
University of California, San Diego

Laura McPherson
Dartmouth College

Shaftesbury Road, Cambridge CB2 8EA, United Kingdom

One Liberty Plaza, 20th Floor, New York, NY 10006, USA

477 Williamstown Road, Port Melbourne, VIC 3207, Australia

314–321, 3rd Floor, Plot 3, Splendor Forum, Jasola District Centre, New Delhi – 110025, India

103 Penang Road, #05–06/07, Visioncrest Commercial, Singapore 238467

Cambridge University Press is part of Cambridge University Press & Assessment, a department of the University of Cambridge.

We share the University's mission to contribute to society through the pursuit of education, learning and research at the highest international levels of excellence.

www.cambridge.org
Information on this title: www.cambridge.org/9781009543583
DOI: 10.1017/9781009543637

© Gabriela Caballero and Laura McPherson 2025

This publication is in copyright. Subject to statutory exception and to the provisions of relevant collective licensing agreements, no reproduction of any part may take place without the written permission of Cambridge University Press & Assessment.

When citing this work, please include a reference to the DOI 10.1017/9781009543637

First published 2025

A catalogue record for this publication is available from the British Library

ISBN 978-1-009-54358-3 Hardback
ISBN 978-1-009-54362-0 Paperback
ISSN 2633-9064 (online)
ISSN 2633-9056 (print)

Cambridge University Press & Assessment has no responsibility for the persistence or accuracy of URLs for external or third-party internet websites referred to in this publication and does not guarantee that any content on such websites is, or will remain, accurate or appropriate.

For EU product safety concerns, contact us at Calle de José Abascal, 56, 1°, 28003 Madrid, Spain, or email eugpsr@cambridge.org

Phonology in Language Documentation

Elements in Phonology

DOI: 10.1017/9781009543637
First published online: October 2025

Gabriela Caballero
University of California, San Diego

Laura McPherson
Dartmouth College

Author for correspondence: Gabriela Caballero, gcaballero@ucsd.edu

Abstract: This Element addresses the challenges and opportunities that arise in the study of sound systems of understudied languages within the context of language documentation, an expanding field that seeks to develop records of the world's languages and their patterns of use in their broader cultural and social context. The topics covered in this Element focus on different elements of language documentation and their relationship to phonological analysis, including lexicography, documentary corpora, music and the verbal arts, as well as grammar writing. For each of these areas, the authors examine methodological and theoretical implications for phonology. With growing concern in the field of language documentation and linguistics more generally for the distribution and implementation of the products of research and its impact on Indigenous language communities, this Element also discusses how phonological documentation may contribute to the development of resources for language communities.

Keywords: documentary corpora, music, verbal arts and music, ethics and community goals, phonological theory and typology

© Gabriela Caballero and Laura McPherson 2025

ISBNs: 9781009543583 (HB), 9781009543620 (PB), 9781009543637 (OC)
ISSNs: 2633-9064 (online), 2633-9056 (print)

Contents

1 Introduction — 1

2 Lexicography — 10

3 Documentary Corpus — 16

4 Music and the Verbal Arts — 26

5 Grammar Writing — 32

6 Phonological Documentation and Community Goals — 38

7 Conclusion — 42

References — 44

1 Introduction

Language documentation is a novel and expanding area that focuses on the making and keeping of records of the world's languages and their patterns of use in their broader cultural, social, and historical context. Within this broader perspective, the study of phonological patterns of understudied languages raises unique methodological and analytical questions for the field of phonology. This Element addresses some of these questions, examining methods in phonological data collection, tools, and best practices in the assembly of documentary corpora for phonological analysis, as well as interdisciplinary approaches to documentation of phonological systems. It also examines the challenges and opportunities that arise for those interested in bringing data from documentary corpora to bear on typological and theoretical questions in the field of phonology. Crucially, as the field of language documentation and linguistics more generally is concerned with the distribution and implementation of the products of research and its impact on speakers and signers in language communities, this Element also discusses how phonological documentation may contribute to the development of resources for language communities.

In the rest of this introduction, we address two critical questions: (i) What is language documentation? and (ii) Why should we be concerned with phonological data and analysis within the context of language documentation?

1.1 What Is Language Documentation?

Documentary linguistics is "concerned with the methods, tools, and theoretical underpinnings for compiling a representative and lasting multipurpose record of a natural language or one of its varieties" (Gippert et al. 2006: v; Himmelmann 1998, 2006). Its primary goal is to represent a wide range of instances and types of language use in their social, cultural, and ecological contexts. As a field, language documentation developed in response to a series of factors, including: (i) concerns about the threats to the world's linguistic diversity and impacts of language loss on the field of linguistics, allied scholarly fields, and Indigenous communities; (ii) the development of data recording and processing technologies that allow for the creation and long-term maintenance of multimodal language corpora; (iii) a focus on interdisciplinary approaches that seek a holistic study of human language, with special attention to the cultural and ecological dimensions of language practices in language communities; and (iv) growing awareness and recognition of community-based perspectives and priorities in the development of documentary corpora.

Modern language documentation has its roots in the Americanist linguistic tradition of Franz Boas, though its present-day iteration is the result of decades of evolution (Woodbury 2011). Boas viewed linguistics as a branch of ethnology (Boas 1911), and as such, language and linguistic structure were inexorably intertwined with culture, beliefs, verbal art, and other areas of discourse. To document this interrelated set of practices, Boas advocated for the creation of his famous "trilogy": a descriptive grammar, a corpus of texts, and a dictionary. In the original Boasian tradition, no one product was more important than any other; rather, they each supported and built on one another. Boas was also ahead of his time in his commitment to involving native speakers in the research and publication process (Woodbury 2011), though he also subscribed to the idea that the Indigenous languages and cultures of North America were destined to disappear (Garrett 2023). As discussed in further detail in Section 6, language documentation as a field seeks to move past this legacy and develop a new paradigm where Indigenous language communities' priorities and needs are central in documentary projects and where language documentation can support language sustainability.

As the twentieth century progressed, trends in the field changed. First, the pendulum swung away from a focus on language as a system integrated with culture and speaker use, as generative traditions that emphasized abstract linguistic structure to be the main goal of linguistic inquiry dominated the latter half of the twentieth century. In the 1980s, so-called descriptive linguistics (Himmelmann 1998) arose, in which the greatest value was placed on the descriptive grammar, with texts coming to be viewed as simply "raw materials" rather than an integral part of linguistic documentation. As the scale of global language endangerment entered the consciousness of the field of linguistics (Hale et al. 1992), the 1990s sowed the seeds of the modern field of language documentation. This was coupled with significant technological advances that made recording, transcribing, and archiving a documentary corpus far more feasible than ever before.

Today, language documentation shows echoes of Franz Boas' original philosophy of language inquiry, with the goal being "the integration of the study of language structure, language use, and the culture of language" (Hill 2006a: 113). Some of the key aspects of documentary linguistics may be summarized as follows (Himmelmann 1998, 2006; Woodbury 2003; Hill 2006a; Holton 2018):

- Building upon the assumption that language communities are not linguistically homogeneous but are rather "organizations of diversity," the goal of language documentation is to represent the variation attested in these communities, which may manifest both in terms of different types of language structures and different patterns of use (Hill 2006a).

- The scope of research is broadened by considering the goals and priorities that the "rightsholders" of the output of language documentation – that is, the communities that claim these languages as part of their patrimony – may have in language documentation. The documentary record is shaped by a cultural and ethnographic understanding of language, with the deep involvement of communities. This deep involvement includes paying attention to language ideologies in contexts of language endangerment in order to support what members of Indigenous language communities may truly desire in terms of language resources as the products of documentation (Hinton 2014; Hill 2006b).
- The documentarian seeks to record the most heterogeneous sample of naturally occurring speech genres (conversations, monologues, narratives, myths, ceremonial speeches, etc.) that may be relevant and attested in a language community; controlled elicited linguistic data may also be part of the record, but there is a much broader scope beyond recording data to address specific analytical questions under investigation.
- With its concern for a holistic study of language, language documentation is inherently interdisciplinary, requiring collaboration with scholars in fields such as astronomy, ethnography, biology, sociolinguistics, geology, and linguistic anthropology, among other disciplines (Holton 2018). The products of language documentation are also ideally useful to the widest range of scholarly disciplines.
- "Data" is at the center stage: Analyses of linguistic patterns and phenomena are ideally linked to language corpora, which makes it possible to make linguistic analyses more accountable and transparent; crucially, there is concern for ethical use and maintenance of documentary data that adhere to principles of Indigenous Data Sovereignty, respecting the protocols, needs, and sociopolitical realities of speech communities (Holton et al. 2022).
- The language documentarian tries to anticipate what various communities, academic and nonacademic, may need from the documentary record in 100 years (or more) from when the record is created (Woodbury 2003).

These different dimensions give language documentation the ability to raise important questions and bring about unique opportunities for the development of linguistic typology and theory. In this Element, we focus on the methodological and theoretical dimensions that are relevant in the study of phonological systems within the context of language documentation. We note that this encompasses both the study of sound systems of spoken language varieties and phonological systems of signed (sign) language varieties. Here we focus on the former, given our research on spoken languages. For references on documentary and descriptive linguistics of signed languages and ethnographic methods in sign language studies, see Fischer (2009), Nyst (2015), Padden (2015), Rarrick and Wilson (2016), Hou (2017, 2020), Hochgesang (2019), and Kusters and Hou (2020). For work focusing on the documentation and revitalization of signed languages in American Indian communities, see McKay-Cody (1996), Davis and McKay-Cody (2010), and Bickford and McKay-Cody (2018). For a comprehensive overview of signed language corpora, see Fenlon and Hochgesang (2022). For references focusing on the phonology of sign languages in the context of language documentation, see Nyst et al. (2003), Hou (2018), Nyst (2019), and Morgan (2022).[1]

1.2 Why Phonology in Language Documentation?

In order to achieve these multifaceted goals and to serve a wide range of stakeholders, language documentation cannot simply be a stockpile of unanalyzed recordings. Rather, to ensure documentary materials are usable by communities and linguists alike, they require transcriptions and translations, both of which require linguistic analysis. Arguably most important is phonological analysis. Consider the act of transcription. Without phonology, we would not have a phonemic analysis of the language. Transcriptions would remain at a surface phonetic level, missing crucial relationships between forms and making the materials much harder to use both for linguists and for speakers, who are unlikely to be consciously aware of allophonic variation, especially at the postlexical level (Mohanan 1982; Snider 2014).

Beyond transcription, phonemic and phonological analysis form the foundation of all other linguistic analysis. Indeed, phonology permeates the grammar, as is evident from extensive work on the interfaces with morphology (e.g., Kiparsky 1985; Inkelas 1997; Booij 2000; Anttila 2002; Inkelas 2014) and syntax (e.g., Truckenbrodt 2007; Elordieta 2008; Selkirk 2011; Seidl 2013).[2] Unfortunately, phonology is often treated simply as a stepping stone to other forms of analysis rather than being treated as a topic of deeper study in its own right. This can be seen in the comparatively few pages dedicated to phonology in many descriptive grammars (see discussion in Rice 2014). And yet, language documentation and description offer phonologists the opportunity to gain

---

[1] Other research on phonological patterns of signed languages based on more traditional methods of elicitation include Zeshan (2000) on Indo-Pakistani Sign Language, Nyst (2007) on Adamorobe Sign Language from Ghana, Marsaja (2008) on Kata Kolok from Indonesia, and Schmaling (2000) on Hausa Sign Language from Nigeria (all references cited in Morgan 2022).

[2] The literature on both of these interfaces is vast and far outside the scope of this current work. For further references on the phonology–morphology interface, see Inkelas (2014); for the syntax–phonology interface, see Selkirk (2011) and Newell (2018).

a more comprehensive view of the phonological system than could be achieved through targeted elicitation alone.[3] Conversely, greater attention to phonology offers a number of benefits in building a documentary corpus.

First, language documentation's focus on multiple genres of speech and different kinds of language materials can reveal unique phonological phenomena. For instance, building a lexical database can uncover sound symbolic tendencies (Blasi et al. 2016; Kawahara et al. 2019; Kawahara 2020), especially when considering specialized lexical domains such as flora–fauna vocabulary (e.g., Döhler 2018; Badenoch 2019) or ideophones (e.g., Dingemanse 2012). Naturalistic texts provide a much better source of data for studying prosody than elicitation could, especially if a phonologist does not think to elicit certain prosodically marked structures such as vocatives and discourse markers. Certain phenomena like ideophones and interjections (Dingemanse 2012; Lee 2017), which can display exceptional phonological behavior, can be difficult to elicit and are much more prevalent in texts.

Second, most language documentarians are interested in the analysis of a language's grammar as a whole, and this wide-sweeping perspective offers deeper insights into the phonological system. We offer an example from the second author's work on the Seenku (Mande; Burkina Faso) tone system. The language has four phonemic tone levels, but it was only the behavior of these tones in morphological alternations such as plural formation (McPherson 2017a) and verbal inflection that provided evidence of sub-phonemic tone features in their phonological representation (McPherson 2017b).

Third, the relationship between phonology and language documentation and description is symbiotic, with a focus on phonology likewise providing a more comprehensive understanding of the grammatical system as a whole. To continue with the theme of tone, in languages with extensive grammatical tone such as Otomanguean (Palancar 2016) or Bantu languages (Odden & Bickmore 2014), insufficient attention paid to tonal analysis would mean an incomplete understanding of the language's morphosyntax.

Finally, the pursuit of phonological evidence can lead to the inclusion of genres in language documentation that may otherwise be overlooked. This includes music, as we will discuss later in this Element, but also poetry and language games (Fitzgerald 2017; Campbell 2020; Agostinho & Araujo 2021; Epps et al. 2023).

---

[3] This is not to disparage (phonological) elicitation, which complements work with large corpora and plays an important role in probing speaker judgments, filling in gaps in the database, and providing negative evidence, among other things. For a discussion of the importance of hypothesis testing and elicitation in morphosyntactic fieldwork, see Davis et al. (2014).

In short, phonology and language documentation go hand in hand; language documentation presents a wide range of data sources for phonological analysis, while a phonologist's goals and perspective diversify the assembly of a documentary corpus and can deepen our understanding of a language's grammatical system. Our goal in this Element is to encourage this symbiosis through a discussion of methodologies and theoretical implications, as well as considering how phonology in language documentation can serve a community's needs and interests.

1.3 Methods, Languages, and Communities

The intersection of phonological research and language documentation involves an immense range of phenomena, methods, language contexts, and theoretical implications. As alluded to above, in this Element we draw on our own research experiences with spoken languages. We provide further details on what phenomena, languages, and language communities shape our perspective and research as phonologists and documentarists, and we discuss how the methods and questions addressed in this Element may be applied to a wider range of language and community contexts.

In terms of our research in phonology, we have investigated patterns and phenomena related to tone, musical surrogates, prosodic structure, and phonology and its interfaces, among other topics. We have carried out this research within the context of long-term documentary projects with members of language communities where a full range of registers and genres are attested, including Choguita Rarámuri (Uto-Aztecan; Northern Mexico), San Juan Piñas Mixtec (Otomanguean; Southern Mexico and California), and Seenku (Mande; Burkina Faso). We provide some details about the development of these projects and the resulting documentary materials on which we base our scholarship.

Choguita Rarámuri is a language spoken by approximately 1,000 people in the Sierra Tarahumara, which is part of the Madre Occidental in Northern Mexico. The documentary corpus of this language has been developed by the first author together with Choguita Rarámuri community members over the past two decades.[4] This corpus consists of over 200 hours of audio and video recordings and is heterogeneous in terms of genres, with recordings of naturalistic speech such as conversations; procedural texts; personal, historical, and procedural narratives; monolingual interviews with elders by younger speakers; and prayers and ceremonial speech, among other genres. The naturalistic genres

---

[4] The documentary corpus comprises two collections archived at the Endangered Languages Archive (ELAR) (Caballero 2015) and at UC Berkeley's California Language Archive (CLA) (Chaparro Gardea et al. 2019).

are complemented by data from different kinds of controlled elicitation, including elicitation using experimental methods to obtain specific data for phonological and morphophonological analysis, as well as more traditional methods to elucidate grammatical patterns for the completion of a reference grammar (Caballero 2022a). The corpus is also heterogeneous in terms of contributors, with recordings of thirty-four language-expert participants representing differences in age, gender, varying levels of bilingualism, and social role in the community.[5]

San Juan Piñas Mixtec (Tò'ōn Ndá'ví) is a previously undocumented Otomanguean language spoken by approximately 300 people in Oaxaca, Mexico and a larger number of speakers in diaspora communities in California and other places in the United States and Mexico. The first author is part of a team led by L1 speaker Claudia Juárez Chávez that, since 2020 and in collaboration with other community members and linguistics faculty and students, has sought to analyze and document the language. While the documentation and analysis of the language is intended for both community and academic audiences, the goals of language community members are central in shaping the documentary agenda and access to outcomes of the research. Documentary materials recorded so far in San Juan Piñas, Oaxaca, and San Diego county include in situ recordings of cultural and ecological knowledge, procedural narratives, interviews, historical narratives, and conversations, in addition to elicited materials focusing on linguistic analysis. Additional outcomes of the project so far include lexical resources for a multimedia trilingual talking dictionary designed for speakers and learners of the language (Juárez Chávez et al. 2022) and analytical writings focusing on the tonal and morphosyntactic properties of the language (Duarte Borquez 2023; Caballero et al. 2024; Caballero et al. in press, Duarte Borquez et al. in press). A documentary deposit of a subset of materials is underway at the California Language Archive (Juárez Chávez et al. in press).

Seenku is a Northwestern Mande language spoken in Burkina Faso by approximately 15,000 people. The second author has led a documentation project on the language since 2013, which has resulted in a corpus of over 300 hours, including an extensive longitudinal and cross-sectional corpus of children's language acquisition (McPherson 2018a; McPherson in press, a, b). In addition, the corpus comprises a wide variety of genres, including vocal and

---

[5] The project initially developed from an interest in conducting linguistic research for a doctoral dissertation by the first author and the goal of establishing a long-term relationship with community members interested in language and cultural documentation; the scope of the project was eventually shaped by Choguita community members interested in documentation and creating a community-based record of language, cultural, and artistic practices.

instrumental music, procedural narratives, interviews across different ages and dialects, and naturalistic conversations, as well as traditional elicitation with several different speakers. The corpus is accompanied by a reference grammar (McPherson 2020) and a lexical database of nearly 1,700 headwords (a version of which can be found in the RefLex database, https://reflex.cnrs.fr/)

In this Element, we discuss several case studies drawing from our own work in these projects, as well as work reported in the literature from a variety of languages and phenomena that are similarly grounded in language documentation methods and/or intensive fieldwork with language communities where languages are used in everyday life by their speakers. Given our research focus on tone and other prosodic phenomena, this Element provides multiple case studies and examples relating to these phenomena. This focus on tone and prosody is especially relevant in the context of language documentation, as these are phenomena that (i) have historically been understudied and (ii) are very active at the interfaces with morphology and syntax and are thus of utmost importance to a holistic understanding of the grammatical system. We note, however, that the methods described in this Element are more generally applicable beyond tonal and prosodic phenomena and may also be extended to investigating phenomena involving segmental phonological structure (see, for instance, work by Myriam Lapierre on the segmental and prosodic structure of Panãra, Mẽbêngôkre, and other languages of the Jê family (Brazil) [Lapierre 2023a, 2023b, 2023c; Huff & Lapierre 2021], which is based on methodologies that combine structured elicitation, text annotation, lexicographic work, and participant observation within the context of extensive fieldwork and language documentation in the Brazilian Amazon).

These case studies also focus on investigating phonological patterns through examination of data stemming from large, heterogeneous corpora that include naturally occurring speech. One question that therefore arises is how widely applicable can the methods of documentary linguistics for phonological research be with languages that exhibit varying degrees of vitality?[6] The documentary methods we outline here may be implemented with languages that exhibit a higher degree of attrition. In particular, documentation may be undertaken alongside revitalization and reclamation efforts in Indigenous language communities in interventions that seek to advance the sustainability of these languages and support the emergence of new generations of speakers (Carpenter et al. 2021). An example of this is found in the documentation of Cahuilla, a Uto-Aztecan language of the Takic branch

---

[6] We thank an anonymous reviewer for raising this important question.

spoken in Southern California with interrupted intergenerational transmission of the language. While Cahuilla has been documented in past decades (Seiler 1965, 1970, 1977; Seiler & Hioki 1979; Sauvel & Munro 1981), these records mainly reflect elicited data. New documentation carried out by Ray Huaute with two L1 master elder speakers supplemented earlier documentary records with new recordings of conversations, traditional ecological knowledge, contemporary tribal histories and family lineages, and place names and their ecological and cultural context, among other genres, which resulted in a contemporary documentary collection of Cahuilla (Huaute 2020). This novel documentation also involved enriching previously recorded materials of the Cahuilla language with translations and cultural and linguistic annotations of these materials. The new materials are designed to support language reclamation, combining novel data with archival materials and the development of analytical materials, which include the description and analysis of the phonology and morphology of the language (Huaute 2022, 2023).

Beyond the specifics of each language and community context, and as discussed in Section 6, we advocate for adopting protocols that advance the priorities and interests of language communities in language documentation and that are consistent with principles of Indigenous Data Sovereignty (Rainie et al. 2019).

1.4 Structure of This Element

In the remainder of this Element, we focus on different elements of language documentation and their relationship to phonological analysis. In Section 2, we examine lexicography and the important role it plays in phonemic analysis as well as the exploration of stochastic phonological patterns. In Section 3, we turn to documentary corpora, the heart of language documentation. A documentary corpus provides crucial data on naturalistic connected speech and phonological variation, as well as higher-level phonology, including intonation, postlexical processes, and phonology's interfaces with morphology and syntax. Section 4 focuses on music and the verbal arts, where the artistic adaptation of language can elucidate aspects of phonological structure as well as speakers' metalinguistic awareness of it. Section 5 considers the relationship between grammar writing and phonology in the context of language documentation, where examples are drawn from a large recorded (and ideally accessible) text corpus. We also consider how phonological description can be interwoven throughout a grammar with traditional ascending structure (phonology > morphology > syntax > discourse, etc.), thus putting the focus on how phonology functions in the language as a whole rather than being treated simply as a building block toward higher levels of grammar. In Section 6, we discuss the place of phonology in service of language pedagogy and other community goals, focusing on the importance of phonemic analysis, phonological variation, and orthography development. Finally, in Section 7, we consider the future of language documentation and phonology.

2 Lexicography

Lexicography, the practice of compiling dictionaries, has a long history in language description and documentation, being one of the three core elements of the Boasian trilogy of "dictionary – texts – grammar." Of course, it has an even longer history outside of language documentation, indeed dating back thousands of years, with Sumerian cuneiform tablets of word lists (Hartmann 1986). Today, lexicography can be considered its own field, separate from language documentation or even mainstream linguistics, with its own methodologies, journals, and traditions. As Grimm (2022) points out, lexicography for well-resourced languages can differ greatly from lexicography in the context of language documentation of understudied languages, in terms of methodological considerations (e.g., the grammar of widely spoken languages is already well understood, and there are often huge datasets to draw from) as well as audiences and intended use (e.g., monolingual literate classroom settings vs. language reclamation and revitalization contexts).

In the context of language documentation, lexicography typically goes hand in hand with text collection and corpus building, which we discuss further in Section 3. As texts are transcribed, new words are added to the lexicon, and these entries can be accompanied by example sentences drawn from the texts. Building a lexicon together with text collection has the added benefit of seeing words in context (phonological, morphosyntactic, semantic, and discourse), which not only furthers morphophonological analysis – crucial for deciding which form or forms to use as the headword in the lexicon – but also provides a deeper understanding of the meaning of a word and its patterns of use. The lexicon can also be expanded through elicitation or translation-based work. For instance, Mosel (2011) describes a process of building thematic mini dictionaries by choosing a semantic domain (often of cultural relevance) and working with the community to identify vocabulary related to the topic through a variety of methods. For good overviews of lexicography in language documentation, including methodology, see Haviland (2006), Mosel (2011), Rice (2018), Grimm (2022), and van der Berg (2024). Finally, lexicography is an area well suited to the interdisciplinary nature of language documentation, given the extensive cultural and ecological knowledge stored in a language's lexicon. For discussion of interdisciplinary collaborative approaches, see, for example, Si (2011), Evans (2012), Baksh-Comeau and Winer (2016), Brown et al. (2017), and Amith (2020).

2.1 Lexicography and Phonological Analysis

The utility of lexicography to phonological analysis cannot be understated. A critical tool in phonemic analysis is the minimal pair, two words with just a single phonological difference in the same location and with different meanings. Put simply, to identify minimal pairs, we need words – preferably a lot of them – and their meanings. On a smaller scale, this is often where targeted, elicitation-based descriptive linguistics begins: with the collection of word lists. However, these word lists have a range of limitations that more complete lexicography helps to overcome. First and most obviously, lexical elicitation that does not aim to produce a lexicon will typically result in a smaller set of lexical items, which means fewer opportunities to find minimal pairs and/or marginal phonemes. Second, traditional word lists, such as Swadesh lists, tend to skew toward concrete lexical items, often nouns, which are easier to elicit.[7] Phonotactic patterns and even phoneme inventory are known to differ between syntactic categories (Smith 2011; Gouskova 2018), making it important to have ample representation of different categories (though nouns do tend to show the widest range of phonological contrasts). See Section 2.3 for further discussion on theoretical uses of lexical databases.

The relationship between lexicography and phonology is symbiotic. While the lexicon offers the phonologist a wealth of data to identify phonological patterns, both segmental and suprasegmental, the very structure of lexical entries requires a firm understanding of the language's morphophonology or even morphosyntax. In many languages, the underlying form of a word or morpheme cannot be determined in isolation (consider the classic case of German or Russian final devoicing – an inflected form is required to determine the underlying voicing of the final obstruent); and if one accepts the notion of abstract underlying representations (such as the Underlying Representation [UR] /ætam/ as the root morpheme in both English *atom* and *atomic*), then there are cases in which no single surface form of a word contains all necessary information to determine its underlying form.[8] Even if a word has been identified through working with a text corpus and not through isolated translation, further elicitation should place the word in different phonological and morphosyntactic contexts. This process helps to identify its underlying form or, for those who reject the notion of underlying forms, to identify any alternations or

---

[7] As an anonymous reviewer points out, the purpose of a Swadesh list is not to probe the phonological system but rather to explore language relatedness, and so a focus on concrete lexical items is appropriate in that context. The point remains, though, that this offers only a very limited set of data for phonological analysis.

[8] For discussion of the theoretical status of underlying forms and their validity, see e.g. Krämer (2018) or Hyman (2018).

sandhi patterns; these elicited frame sentences can also help provide simple example sentences for the dictionary if the naturalistic occurrence in the text corpus is particularly long or complicated.

In the next section, we offer a case study from the second author's work with Seenku (Mande; Burkina Faso), where morphophonological analysis, with the aid of targeted elicitation, proved crucial for decisions on how to structure lexical entries. While this case study involves tonal patterns, we note that the insights and conclusions may be extended to segmental phonological patterns. This constitutes a case in which phonology and phonological analysis aids language documentation; for cases in which the lexicon serves as a critical source of data for phonological analysis (i.e., cases where language documentation aids phonology), see Section 2.3.

2.2 Case Study: Argument-Head Tone Sandhi in Seenku (Mande; Burkina Faso)

Seenku is a Mande language in the Samogo family spoken by around 15,000 people in southwestern Burkina Faso. It has a highly complex tone system, with four contrastive levels (called Extra-low X, Low L, High H, and Super-high S), which can combine on single syllables to create numerous contour tones; see also Section 4.1 for how music has helped in the phonemic analysis of this tone system. The language displays a process of grammatically conditioned tone sandhi, wherein the internal argument can trigger tonal alternations on a head noun, postposition, or verb. This process of "argument-head tone sandhi" (McPherson 2019a) poses a challenge for lexicography, since Seenku syntax dictates that the categories involved (inalienable nouns, postpositions, and transitive verbs) appear obligatorily with an argument, but the tone of the argument almost always has an effect on the head word's tone.

We will focus here on verbs, which are unique among the categories subject to argument-head tone sandhi in that sandhi only applies when the verb is in its irrealis form. In the realis, there is no interaction between the object and verb, but other tonal morphology applies that obscures the underlying tone. We find three tonal categories of transitive verbs, which we illustrate here with 'hit', 'sell,' and 'buy'. All three verbs surface as S-toned after an S-toned argument:

(1) mí bǎ̰   'hit us'   (S)
     mí sɔ̌ɔ   'sell us' (S)
     mí sǎ̰   'buy us'   (S)

Both 'hit' and 'sell' surface as X-toned after a H-toned argument, but 'buy' surfaces as S-toned.

Table 1 Realis forms of three Seenku verbs (representing different tonal classes).

	Progressive	**Perfective**	**Perfect**
'hit'	bá̰ nḛ́ (S)	bá̰ (H)	bä̰ (SX)
'buy'	sɔ́ɔ nḛ́ (S)	sɔ́ɔ (H)	sɔ̈ɔ (SX)
'sell'	sà̰ nḛ́ (L)	sa̰ (X)	sà̰ä̰ (LSX)

(2) mó bä̰ 'hit me' (X)
    mó sɔ̈ɔ 'sell me' (X)
    mó sá̰ 'buy me' (S)

The three verbs are all distinct after an X-toned argument, with 'hit' surfacing as H, 'sell' surfacing as X, and 'buy' surfacing as L while simultaneously raising the argument's tone to L:

(3) ä bá̰ 'hit him/her' (H)
    ä sɔ̈ɔ 'sell him/her' (X)
    à sà̰ 'buy him/her' (L)

In realis contexts, 'hit' and 'sell' pattern together, surfacing as S-toned in the progressive, H-toned in the perfective, and SX-toned in the perfect (where the umlaut marks an SX contour). The verb 'buy,' on the other hand, surfaces as L-toned in the progressive,[9] X-toned in the perfective, and LSX-toned in the perfect (with vowel lengthening to host the tri-tone contour). These outputs are shown in Table 1.

What, then, does one put as the headword in a dictionary? There is but one cell of the paradigm where all three are distinct (in the irrealis with an X-toned light argument[10]), but the differences in this form are subtle both acoustically and typographically (consider *ä sɔ̈ɔ* vs. *à sà̰*). It also is not a good representation of what could be considered the abstract underlying form of the verb, which can be deduced by comparison with a marginal possessive construction with alienable nouns that undergo the same sandhi process, but which – by virtue of being alienable – are able to surface in isolation and thus display their lexical tone. From this comparison, we can say with some confidence that 'hit' is underlyingly S-toned (/bá̰/), 'sell' is

---

[9] The surface L tone is the result of simplifying an LS contour before an S-toned particle.

[10] Light arguments have the phonological shape V or N, which is only found in pronouns. Canonical CV pronouns and non-pronominal arguments have slightly different tonal behavior; see McPherson (2019a) for further discussion.

underlying H-toned (/sɔ́ɔ/), and 'buy' is underlyingly X-toned (/sà̤/). However, these are at best abstract underlying representations, and it is unclear whether Seenku-speaking dictionary users would recognize them. For a Seenku learner or a linguist using the lexicon, including only these abstract underlying forms would require the computation of the correct surface form in both the realis and irrealis. But the patterns are indeed predictable, and so including all of these different paradigm cells would be an inefficient use of space, especially if one considers making a printed dictionary.

Ultimately, the second author made the decision to include two surface forms for every verb: the three-way distinct cell with the pronominal argument *ä*, but preceded by the progressive form (e.g., *bǎ̤ nɛ̰́, sɔ́ɔ nɛ̰́, sà̤ nɛ̰́*), which better allows for alphabetizing while also representing the underlying split between higher-toned verbs /bǎ̤/ and /sɔ́ɔ/ versus lower-toned verbs like /sà̤/. These are surface forms, but at the same time, by considering the two forms together, they unambiguously point to the tonal class; this allows for the computation of all other surface forms, like principal parts in the Classicist tradition. Others working on the language could come to different decisions, and other languages may present even more complicated cases requiring more principal parts to fully capture a word's morphophonological behavior. But as this example shows, accurately representing a lexical entry is dependent on phonological analysis, which can extend far beyond the word itself. Even determining an underlying form, or perhaps more accurately a phonological class, requires studying the morphosyntax, showing that once again taking a holistic view of a language's phonology is crucial – and an opportunity more readily offered in the context of language documentation.

2.3 Implications for Theoretical Phonology and Phonological Analysis

Many of today's advances in phonological theory leverage lexical databases, recognizing that many phonological generalizations are stochastic in nature. This patterned variation in the lexicon has been shown to be part of phonological grammar, with the results of wug testing (Berko 1958) closely matching frequency patterns among existing lexical items (Coleman & Pierrehumbert 1997; Zuraw 2000; Frisch & Zawaydeh 2001; Albright 2002; Hayes & Londe 2006; Becker 2009; Zymet 2018, among many others). For example, Hayes and Londe (2006) found that rates of backness harmony among stems in the Hungarian lexicon are mirrored when asked to apply harmony to nonce stems. This area of inquiry has driven the development and refinement of stochastic phonological models, such as stochastic optimality theory (Boersma 1998; Boersma & Hayes 2001), Noisy Harmonic Grammar (Boersma & Pater 2008/2016), and Maximum Entropy Harmonic Grammar (Goldwater & Johnson 2003; Hayes & Wilson 2008) while also theorizing on the role of lexically indexed constraints (Coetzee 2009; Pater 2010). Though most of the studies cited here do not come from the realm of language documentation, they demonstrate the importance of a dictionary or lexical database – products of language documentation – for phonological analysis.

In addition to studying stochastic and gradient processes, a lexicon also allows us to probe the phonological system of a language by calculating the functional load of different phonemic contrasts. The functional load of a contrast (for instance, between /t/ and /d/) has been argued to have implications for phonological acquisition (Pye et al. 1987; Van Severen et al. 2012), change (Martinet 1952; Hockett 1966; Wedel et al. 2013), and alternations (Lin 2019); for further discussion and cross-linguistic comparison, see Oh et al. (2015). While most studies of functional load still rely on large-scale lexica and corpora, even smaller lexical databases produced in the context of language documentation can begin to address these questions.

We will highlight here two cases where small-scale lexical databases have yielded significant insights for phonological analysis. We take first Shih's (2017) study of Dioula d'Odienne tone patterns. Many studies have shown the existence of cumulative ganging in constraint-based models of phonology, with disagreement about whether such ganging ought to be handled by constraint conjunction (Baković 2000; Itô and Mester 2003; Łubowicz 2005; Smolensky 2006) or by the cumulative ganging of weighted constraints in a Harmonic Grammar model (Farris-Trimble 2008; Pater 2016; Potts et al. 2010). Shih (2017) explores the issue through the lens of a definite–indefinite tonal alternation in Dioula d'Odienne, a Mande variety spoken in northern Côte d'Ivoire. Nouns fall into one of two patterns with respect to the definiteness alternation: Type 1 L.L nouns surface as L.H, while Type 2 L.L nouns surface as H.H; a similar pattern is found with H.H nouns, wherein Type 1 surface in the definite as H.LH while Type 2 surface as L.H. Importantly for the discussion at hand, she draws on data from Braconnier and Diaby's (1982) lexicon of the language, which contains 1,194 nouns marked for which tonal pattern they belong to. As Braconnier (1982) notes, the likelihood of a noun belonging to Type 1 or Type 2 depends on the sonority of the medial C, the similarity of the two vowels, and the nasality of the final vowel and medial consonant. Shih uses the lexical data to develop an analysis of the tone patterns as a case of parasitic harmony, whereby the more similar the segments in the final VCV are across these various parameters, the more likely the noun is to belong to Type 2. There is a ganging effect among the constraints on different kinds of similarity, but in a novel contribution to the debate on conjunction versus additive weights, Shih shows that the Dioula d'Odienne data require *both*. In short, the patterns are "superadditive"; the combined effect of constraints A and B outweigh their simple sum. This contribution to theoretical phonology was made possible by the lexicographic work of Braconnier and Diaby.

A second case study demonstrates the interconnectedness of lexicography and text collection in language documentation, and how the two can combine to provide a source of data for phonological analysis. Fitzgerald (2017) discusses the importance of including verbal arts in language documentation (see also Section 4), including traditional stories and narratives. As discussed at the beginning of this section, the text corpus is critical in lexicography both for identifying new vocabulary and for the inclusion of naturalistic examples. In her work on Tohono O'odham, an Uto-Aztecan language of Arizona and Northern Mexico, Fitzgerald (2013) looked at example sentences in the dictionary of Mathiot (1973), who meticulously included both their pronunciations in naturalistic connected speech as well as their citation forms. Through this lexical data, she discovered a novel vowel harmony pattern in Tohono O'odham triggered by the vowel /i/ but not other high vowels. While this same result could have been found by looking directly at the text corpus, this is not always readily available; dictionaries – including both their headwords as well as their example sentences – can still offer many opportunities to discover phonological patterns at both the lexical level and phrasal level. We discuss text collection and documentary corpora further in the next section.

3 Documentary Corpus

As discussed in Section 1, there has been a long tradition of working with texts in projects focusing on linguistic description of underdocumented languages. Creating a corpus of texts was indeed foundational in the Americanist tradition in linguistics, a tradition that in the twentieth century produced extensive text collections of Indigenous California languages and other languages of the Americas and the rest of the world.[11] In this Boasian tradition, the goal was

---

[11] For California languages alone, some notable examples include Kroeber's (1900) Cheyenne text collection, Goddard's (1904) Hupa text collection, Sapir's (1911) Yana texts, Harrington's (1932) Karuk texts, Voegelin's (1935) Tübatulabal texts, and Hill and Nolasquez' (1973) Cupeño text collection; see also Garrett (2023) for discussion of language and text documentation in the early twentieth century.

originally to assemble a collection of *written* texts primarily consisting of mythological texts (such as creation myths) and other ethnographic materials, which would then be the basis of linguistic and cultural anthropology inquiry (Woodbury 2003). While there was an explicit focus on both language and culture in this period, reference to language use was rare in the early days of this tradition and remained sparse in more contemporary descriptive works (Hill 2006b).

Within the new paradigm of language documentation, however, language use becomes central. The original conception of the text corpus is significantly expanded by considering the diversity of genres, participants, participant roles, communicative purposes, and other features that may be culturally relevant in particular language varieties (Woodbury 2003). For this purpose, language documentation draws from the methods and principles of the "ethnography of communication," which advocates for the study of language within its sociocultural context, focusing on repertoires of local speech practices or "ways of speaking" (Hymes 1971). A crucial assumption made in this framework is that speech communities are not linguistically homogeneous. The task of the documentarian therefore is to undertake an ethnographic analysis of how speech-act types are distributed across contexts in a speech community, a task that involves exploring what language experts' understanding of speech activity is within their communities (Hill 2006a: 113). As such, each documentary text corpus is a unique reflection of the very specific circumstances and agendas of participants involved in each documentary project.

Finally, in terms of the phonological study of underdocumented languages, there was an initial difficulty with respect to providing an accurate phonetic representation of the sound system in early research, with later developments in the twentieth century achieving greater phonetic accuracy and attention to variation, though with an emphasis on word-level phonology (for discussion, see Rice 2014). With contemporary language documentation, new tools and methods are available to produce state-of-the-art phonological descriptions and analyses of both segmental and suprasegmental phonological patterns and phenomena. Within this context, we may ask: What is needed in a documentation-based corpus for carrying out phonological analysis? We address this question next.

3.1 Phonological Analysis in the Context of Documentation-Based Corpora

According to Currie Hall et al. (2018: 616), a minimal corpus for phonological analysis within the context of fieldwork is "a list of phonologically transcribed words, possibly accompanied by additional information such as their orthographic representation, frequency of use in some body of text, part of speech, etc."[12] In a language documentation project, however, the corpus will include phonologically transcribed and annotated data from a wide range of naturalistic genres of speech, including conversations, narratives, and ritual/ceremonial speech, in addition to controlled elicited data. Ideally, this corpus will also feature the speech of a heterogeneous group of speakers in terms of a number of relevant demographic variables. This heterogeneity of both genres and participants has concrete benefits for the study of phonological patterns for a number of reasons.

First, careful transcription of texts deepens every level of phonological analysis by considering how words and morphemes appear in connected speech. For instance, as discussed in Section 2, there are cases where underlying phonological forms are only discernible from the study of forms in certain phrasal contexts, for example if the relevant phonological contrast is neutralized in phrase-final position or in isolation. An example of this is found in tone systems where some morphemes bear floating tones that are only observable in non-final phrasal contexts. This is the case of Peñoles Mixtec, an Otomanguean language spoken in Mexico where the presence of L(ow) floating tones is only observable when another morpheme follows, for example, a /H.H^L/ noun is realized in isolation as [H.H] ([ñáñá] 'coyote'), since its floating L tone goes unrealized in isolation; however, when followed by a word that lacks a tone in its first syllable, the floating L surfaces to the right on the toneless syllable ([ñáñá d̀itó] 'uncle's coyote') (Daly and Hyman 2007: 168). In addition, Peñoles Mixtec, as documented for other Mixtec language varieties, exhibits complex register effects, including both downstep and upstep.[13] Crucially, these effects are cumulative and unbounded, and discernible only by comparison of different lexical and grammatical tonal sequences in phonological phrases. A carefully transcribed and annotated documentary record can allow the discovery of similar phenomena, which can then be examined through controlled elicitation.

A documentary corpus provides crucial evidence in the study of other patterns and phenomena that are not observable from a list of phonologically transcribed words uttered in isolation, including postlexical phonology and the phonology–syntax interface. As an example of the latter, documentary work on Guébie (Kru; Côte d'Ivoire) reveals a typologically unusual pattern of

---

[12] Currie Hall et al. (2018) discuss this in the context of a computational tool for doing phonological corpus analysis. For further discussion on the use of different types of corpora for phonological analysis, see Currie Hall (2022).

[13] Complex register effects are documented in a number of Mixtec language varieties, including Acatlán Mixtec (Pike and Wistrand 1974; Snider 1988), Coatzospan Mixtec (Pike and Wistrand 1974), Ayutla Mixtec (Herrera Zendejas 2014), San Jerónimo de Xayacatlán (Rueda Chaves 2019), and San Juan Piñas Mixtec (Duarte Borquez et al. 2023).

phonologically conditioned nominal concord, where a class of pronouns and adjectives exhibit agreement with the head noun within the noun phrase (Sande 2019). In particular, third-person pronominal forms referring to nonhumans and adjectives exhibit a phonological form that is dependent on the final vowel of the agreement-controlling noun, as shown in (4) (the agreeing elements are highlighted in boldface and underlined).

(4) Phonological agreement of pronouns with antecedents in Guébie (Sande 2019: 838)[14]

a. kʷal**a**$^{4.2}$ e-^{4} ni=**a**$^{4.2}$ ji^3 **a**^{3} kadɛ$^{3.2}$
   farm   1SG.NOM   see.PFV=3SG.ACC   PART   3SG.NOM   be.big.IPFV
   'Farm. I saw it. It's big.'

b. t**ʊ**^{3} e-^{4} ni=**ʊ**$^{4.2}$ ji^3 **ʊ**^{3} kadɛ$^{3.2}$
   battle   1SG.NOM   see.PFV=3SG.ACC   PART   3SG.NOM   be.big.IPFV
   'Battle. I saw it. It's big.'

As shown in these examples, in the first sentence there is a noun which determines the phonological form of pronominal forms in the following sentences; for example, the noun $kʷala^{4.2}$ 'farm' has an agreeing pronoun a^3, while the noun $tʊ^3$ 'battle' has an agreeing pronoun $ʊ^3$ (Sande 2019: 838).

The discussion in Sande (2019) is illustrated with examples from both elicitation and a corpus of audiovisual materials that include annotated texts comprising various genres (Agodio et al. 2014–15). In terms of its theoretical implications, this case raises questions about the architecture of the grammar, and in particular whether syntactic operations have access to phonological information or whether nominal concord itself may involve a post-syntactic operation (as argued in Kramer 2010 and Norris 2014). Sande adopts the latter approach and provides a post-syntactic analysis of Guébie nominal concord, which addresses both the phonologically conditioned agreement patterns as well as the semantically conditioned agreement patterns attested in the language.

A collection of narratives and other naturally occurring discourse is also crucial in the study of prosodic phenomena, including stress, tone, intonation, and their interaction, as well as the effects of position within specific phrasal contexts on the realization of phonemic contrasts or particular phonological processes. As an example, consider the case of the study of prosody in Uspanteko (K'ichean; Guatemala), a language documented by Ryan Bennett, Meg Harvey, Robert Henderson, and Tomás Alberto Méndez

---

[14] Abbreviations used in these examples include: ACC – accusative; IPFV – imperfective; NOM – nominative; PART – particle; PFV – perfective; SG – singular.

López in collaboration with Uspanteko speakers in Guatemala. A collection of Uspanteko texts compiled by Ryan Bennett, Megan Harvey, Robert Henderson, and Tomás Méndez López is available online at https://bkeej.github.io/TextosUspantekos/#/. Uspanteko is a language with lexical tonal contrasts that exhibits a high degree of variability in terms of its phonetic realization tied to different intonational contexts and discourse structure, as well as lexical and sociolinguistically relevant variation (Bennett et al. 2019, 2022).[15] Bennett et al. (2022: 200) observe that in Uspanteko, as in other languages, "isolation forms may not provide reliable information about lexical tone, because the pitch contours on isolated words can be significantly affected by intonational patterns associated with phrases and utterances." The study of Uspanteko phonology has involved examination of data from a corpus of transcribed narratives (involving approximately 54,000 words), as well as a production study with controlled elicitation of tonal targets in different prosodic and discourse environments. Bennett et al. (2019, 2022) find that lexical tonal contrasts in Uspanteko are neutralized in certain intonational contexts, and that the phonological analysis of lexical tone in this language cannot be done without consideration of intonational phonological patterns. More broadly, this study contributes to our understanding of how tone and intonation interact in individual phonological systems (Poser 1984; Hyman 2011; Gussenhoven 2004; Gordon 2016), and is informed by work that assumes the variability of phonetic realization of phonological patterns may reveal crucial aspects of abstract representations in phonology (Pierrehumbert and Beckman 1988; Ladd 2008). In addition to the potential neutralizing effects that intonational patterns have on lexical tonal contrasts, Bennett et al. (2022) also discuss how the high variability in tonal realization in Uspanteko is a consequence of the low functional load that tone has in the lexical phonology of the language,[16] a finding that is consistent with a body of work that shows that patterns with a higher functional load will have a more robust realization in production (e.g., Lindblom 1986; Baese-Berk and Goldrick 2009; Nelson and Wedel 2017). These findings are relevant for our understanding of how phonological distinctions may condition the acoustic realization of speech sounds in a given variety, and, more broadly, for our understanding of the phonetics–phonology interface.

The availability of transcribed textual data is also crucial for languages with complex morphophonological patterns and processes. An example of this is

---

[15] Bennett et al. (2022) note that Uspanteko exhibits a high degree of lexical variation, which they attribute to widespread multilingualism in the Uspanteko speech community.

[16] In particular, while tone is contrastive in the language, Bennett et al. describe the low functional load of tone as diagnosed by the very few tonal minimal pairs attested in the language.

found in Yoloxóchitl Mixtec, an Otomanguean language spoken in the state of Guerrero, Mexico with complex lexical and grammatical tone patterns. While Yoloxóchitl Mixtec has fewer tone sandhi patterns compared to other Mixtec language varieties (like Peñoles Mixtec, referenced above), it nevertheless exhibits tonological alternations that are dependent on the phonological, morphological, and morphosyntactic context; this is the case in morphotonological alternations attested in pronominal enclitics and patterns of tonal allophony of verbs of different classes (Palancar et al. 2016). The analysis of these patterns is based on examination of data from a large documentary corpus consisting of over 100 hours of transcribed materials, compiled through the documentation project "Corpus and lexicon development: Endangered genres of discourse and domains of cultural knowledge in Tu^{21}un^3 i^{4}sa^{1}bi^{14} ('the Mixtec language') of Yoloxóchitl, Guerrero" led by Jonathan Amith and Rey Castillo García. The documentary materials of Yoloxóchitl Mixtec are deposited at the Endangered Language Archive (ELAR) and the Archive for Languages of Latin American (AILLA) (the ELAR collection is available online at: http://hdl.handle.net/2196/b42c3b44-67c8-438d-8e79-60d9b2f2d85c).

Here, textual data can also be combined with data obtained through controlled elicitation to assess the phonological properties of paradigmatically related words, given that a full paradigm is unlikely to be recorded through textual data alone. Crucially, the availability of data from a text corpus allows the relative frequency of specific morphophonological patterns in a given language variety to be assessed, as well as data that can be revealing in terms of potential optionality of certain processes. This is again exemplified in the analysis of grammatical tone patterns of Yoloxóchitl Mixtec in Palancar et al. (2016), where data from paradigmatically related forms of 554 verbs of different tonal classes elicited in the construction of a large lexical database (comprising 2,192 lexical entries) complemented the data that was obtained from text corpus materials. The combined data sources allowed the authors to identify which tone patterns are more or less frequent in bimoraic verb stems in the language as well as patterns of tonally conditioned allomorphy (Palancar et al. 2016).

Analysis of phonological data from a documentation-based text corpus also makes it possible to uncover patterns of variation across multiple dimensions, whether it involves variation within and/or across speakers or variation associated with the use of multiple varieties in multilingual/multilectal speech communities. Patterns of variation may also be attested in the context of rapid language shift associated with obsolescence processes. A growing interest in understanding patterns of variation in endangered and underdocumented languages has seen the development of methods and analytical tools within the field of language documentation (Hildebrandt et al. 2017; Skilton 2017; Di Carlo et al. 2021; Good 2023).[17] In the context of phonological documentation, the availability of a text corpus allows the distribution and nature of these patterns to be investigated in a nuanced way. An example of this is found in Grimm's (2021) grammar of Gyeli (Bantu A801; Cameroon). In her description of the phonological system, Grimm notes various patterns of distribution and frequency of phonological and phonetic variation in Gyeli, which she attributes to (i) inter- and intra-speaker variation, (ii) influence from unrelated Bantu language varieties, and (iii) dialectal variation, among other factors. Crucially, patterns of segmental and tonal variation are illustrated with examples drawn from the documentary corpus, which includes high-quality annotations of texts of three different genres (folktales, conversations, and autobiographical narratives) that include intonation phrase breaks and extensive annotation carried out in conjunction with Gyeli speakers. The data from texts was supplemented with data obtained from controlled elicitation.

The development of documentary corpora in the context of language documentation interacts with other developments in the field of phonology. A carefully annotated text corpus allows the use of corpus-based methods, which can then inform our understanding of theoretical questions in phonology, as well as discovering new phenomena or furthering our understanding of the role of frequency in the nature and distribution of phonological patterns. In particular, the development of documentation-based corpora goes hand in hand with increased attention in typological and theoretical research in phonology to pair quantitative analyses with the more traditional qualitative approach generally employed in prior research of underdocumented languages. This includes examination of acoustic data for analysis of phonetic and phonological patterns (see Whalen and McDonough 2019 for an overview). As a concrete example of the possibilities that a documentary-based corpus offers for the instrumental analysis of phonological patterns and phenomena, we consider a specific case study next.

3.2 Case Study: Prosodic Structure in Choguita Rarámuri (Uto-Aztecan; Mexico)

As described in Section 1.4, the Choguita Rarámuri corpus is large and diverse in terms of genres and speakers represented. The nature of the Choguita Rarámuri corpus has allowed for the discovery of relevant phenomena in the phonology and morphology of the language, including complex prosodic

---

[17] For an overview of studies of variation in minoritized languages within the context of linguistic fieldwork, see Stanford and Preston (2009).

phonological patterns. Choguita Rarámuri features a hybrid stress and tone system (with a ternary contrast between falling (/HL/, <ô>), low (/L/, <ò>), and high (/H/, <ó>) tones realized in tonic syllables) (Caballero 2011; Caballero and Carroll 2015). In addition to encoding lexical tone, Choguita Rarámuri deploys f0 in its intonation system, resulting in different accommodation strategies when conflicting tones are assigned to the same tone-bearing units by the lexical/morphological and intonational components (Garellek et al. 2015). One important characteristic of this prosodic system is the high degree of variability in terms of the phonetic realization of tonal contrasts (not unlike the case of Uspanteko described in Section 3.1) both within and across speakers, a complexity that only became apparent during the development of the documentary corpus of the language and assessment of naturalistic speech data from a large number of Choguita Rarámuri speakers. While the pitch differences between the tonal categories were clear for some speakers, they were hard to detect impressionistically for others.

These observations were assessed instrumentally in two studies (Caballero and Carroll 2015; Caballero et al. 2022).[18] These analyses revealed that there are relatively small, though reliable, f0 differences between tonal categories, in results comparable to those found for other Uto-Aztecan tonal languages, such as Balsas Nahuatl (Guion et al. 2010). While the distinction between certain tone primitives is reliably attested for all speakers, the differences in pitch can be rather small and in some cases neutralized for others, at least when considering the pitch patterns of tone-bearing syllables (Caballero et al. 2022). Assessment of tone patterns in different intonational contexts reveals, however, that (i) the tonal categories are further distinguished through changes in f0 over a window encompassing syllables neighboring the tone-bearing syllable (Caballero and Carroll 2015; Garellek et al. 2015; Caballero et al. 2022), and (ii) that utterance-final pitch range expands due to the presence of a H% boundary tone for declaratives (Garellek et al. 2015; Caballero et al. 2022). In addition to these f0 patterns, the data from the Choguita Rarámuri text corpus reveals trends in terms of realization of tonal contrasts involving phonation effects for some speakers, including rearticulation exclusive to HL tones for some speakers (e.g., /naˈpô/ → [naˈpóʔò] 'prickly pear') (Aguilar et al. 2015). These preliminary results were also confirmed through analysis of instrumental data, which showed that voice quality indeed helps differentiate the three tone categories of Choguita Rarámuri for at least some speakers (Caballero et al. 2022).

---

[18] In Caballero et al. (2022), the timing and sequencing of lexical and intonational tones were assessed by varying the length of words and phrases and stress location within phonological words and with respect to phrasal boundaries.

As in the Uspanteko case discussed previously, the findings in the Choguita Rarámuri case are relevant to discussions of the role of phonological contrast in the surface phonetic realization of phonological patterns. In the case of Choguita Rarámuri, while the three tonal primitives involve small f0 distinctions, considering voice quality and f0 patterns contributes to the reliable discriminability of the tonal categories in the language, which play an important role in encoding both lexical and grammatical contrasts (Caballero and Carroll 2015; Caballero and German 2021). That the realization of tonal contrasts through pitch and other phonetic means exhibits speaker-dependent variability is also in alignment with studies that have shown that cue weighting may vary by speaker/listener as well as dialect (Brunelle 2009; Brunelle 2012; Kuang and Cui 2018). More generally, this synchronic configuration may reflect the result of a recent diachronic development of the prosodic system from a stress system to a hybrid one through tonogenesis, a change proposed to have taken place in the Oapan and Ahueliacán varieties of Balsas Nahuatl (Guion et al. 2010). These cases thus may be generalizable to other prosodic systems where tonogenesis and retention of lexical stress lead to similar phonological and phonetic configurations.

3.3 Reproducibility in Language Documentation

One important advantage of developing phonological analyses of data stemming from documentation-based corpora is that it is possible to allow different users, academic and community-based scholars alike, to access the data upon which analyses (phonological or other) are based. This involves *reproducibility*, an alternative to true replicability, when the ability to produce new data by recreating research conditions faithfully is not possible, as in cases of work within a language community (Berez-Kroeker et al. 2018).[19] Reproducibility is of central importance in language documentation, given the special attention paid to the structuring and maintenance of primary digital data, which can then be linked to products of linguistic analysis (Mosel 2014, 2018). Within the context of phonological analysis, one way of implementing reproducibility is to provide audio recordings of specific examples in analytical materials or provide links to the documentary corpora where users can find the original materials that substantiate the analyses proposed. This is exemplified with data from the Choguita Rarámuri grammar written by the first author, where a subset of data examples are provided with a hyperlink that directs users to an open access repository of audio recordings (Caballero 2022b). The example in (5) is used in

---

[19] As observed in Berez-Kroeker et al. (2018: 4), "in many fieldwork-based life and social sciences, true replicability is not possible to achieve. [This is because t]he variables contributing to a particular instance of field observation are too hard to control in many cases."

Table 2 Tonal contrasts in Choguita Rarámuri trisyllabic roots.

Tone	Form	Gloss	Source code
HL	napaˈbû	'to get together'	{FLP in243:4:16.8}
L	sikiˈrè	'to cut'	{SFH el1080:13:37.7}
L	naʔˈsòwa	'to stir, mix'	{JLG co1234:8:41.9}
HL	ˈhûmisi	'to take off, PL'	{LEL tx19:1:40.3}
H	wipiˈsó	'to hit with stick'	{SFH el1080:3:55.8}
H	aˈnátʃa	'to endure'	{MFH el1318:19:58.1}

Caballero (2022a) to illustrate the grammatical and prosodic properties of morphosyntactically unmarked polar questions with conversational data stemming from the Choguita Rarámuri documentary corpus. In the same reference, the examples in Table 2 provide examples of tonal contrasts in trisyllabic roots with data from conversations, texts, and elicitation. Each example is provided with a source code (shown here in curly brackets) with a hyperlink that directs users to a page where individual audio files can be downloaded (all forms are part of a repository [Caballero 2022b] that may be found online at https://doi.org/10.5281/zenodo.7268366).[20]

(5) Morphosyntactically unmarked polar questions in Choguita Rarámuri
  a. *pe uˈsànabi?*
    pe   uˈsàni-na=bi?
    just   six-DISTR=just
    'Just in six places?'
    '¿Nomás en seis partes?' {SFH in61:04:37.8}

  b. *ke biˈlé pe ˈtáʃi iˈtéeli ˈònam tʃaˈbè ko?*
    ke   biˈlé   pe   ˈtási   iˈté-li   ˈòna-ame   tʃaˈbè=ko
    NEG   one   NEG   NEG   exist.NEG-PST   cure-PTCP   before=EMPH
    'There was no medicine before?'
    '¿No había medicina antes?' {SFH in61:06:39.6}

This type of linking between the products of grammatical description/analyses and source annotated text corpora is intended to allow users to form their own conclusions about the analyses provided. We add, however, that the desire to make the output of research reproducible cannot be privileged over the requirement to adhere to ethical guidelines and respect for the wishes of individual

---

[20] Each source code provides the initials of contributing speakers and a unique file identifier of the file name that specifies whether the source document in the corpus is a conversation ('co'), a text ('tx'), an interview ('in'), or elicitation ('el'), among other possible document types. Other abbreviations used in these examples include: DISTR – distributive; EMPH – emphatic; NEG – negation; PL – plural; PST – past; PTCP – participial.

contributors and language communities, who may place limits as to how accessible the products of research on their languages should be.

As we discuss further in Sections 5 and 6, supplementing data examples with audio provides an important tool for language learners in contexts of language revitalization and strengthening (Rice 2014). The careful documentation of phonological variation patterns also has positive ramifications in terms of possible uses of the analyzed data, including the development of pedagogical materials that reflect phonological variation among speakers. This is especially important in contexts of language reclamation, where documentary corpora may also include the speech patterns of language learners and users with different degrees of fluency (we discuss this further in Section 6).

One final important methodological point to be made concerns the use of elicited data and data from the documentary corpus: While the examples and case studies discussed so far involve the use of data from elicitation that carefully controls for the phonological parameters that are relevant in the phonological analysis of each language, the documentary corpus developed for these languages was instrumental in the identification of phonological phenomena, their variable realization across speakers and contexts, and the development of ecologically valid stimuli for controlled elicitation.[21]

4 Music and the Verbal Arts

As we discussed in Section 3, one of the goals of a documentary text corpus is the inclusion of multiple genres. This includes those "at the margins of language" (Dingemanse 2018: 4) like music and poetry, which often play with phonological structure and can thus provide unique analytical insights. As a further benefit, in the experience of the second author, speech communities typically value these recordings and may enjoy working with them more than recordings of everyday speech. Of course, language documentation promotes the inclusion of a diverse range of genres even outside of the verbal arts, such as recipes or prayers, which may offer their own unique phonological insights. For purposes of space, we focus here on the verbal arts.

The verbal arts, which we take here to encompass a wide range of genres including poetry, chant, music, and language games, are based on "the manipulation of elements and components of language in relation to one another"

---

[21] The role of ecological validity is also emphasized in Bennett et al. (2019), who assessed the interaction between tone and intonation in Uspanteko though examination of f0 patterns in a corpus of words selected to be representative of the phonological patterns attested in the language vs. words with all sonorant segments. While the latter is standard practice in studies of tone and intonation (see Jun and Fletcher 2014), an all-sonorant word corpus in Uspanteko would have led to prioritizing the phonological profile of highly marginal words in the language.

(Sherzer 2002: 1). Of central importance to this chapter is the manipulation of sound structure. This can manifest itself in multiple ways depending upon the genre. Take, for instance, rhyming poetry, which relies on parallelism in phonological or syllabic structure across positions, typically (though not always, Peust 2014) the rime of a (stressed) syllable (note the non-accidental homophonous terminology). Imperfect rhyme, where the rhyming elements are nonidentical, tends to reveal metalinguistic knowledge of natural phonological classes or perceptual similarity. For example, many German poets treat front rounded and unrounded vowels as equivalent for rhyme (Peust 2014; Knoop et al. 2021); in Celtic, consonants fall into rhyme classes based on sonority (Kern 2015); and in African-American English rap, patterns of imperfect rhyme in coda consonants are based on perceptual similarity (Katz 2015).

Here, we will highlight some methodologies for studying phonology in the documentation of verbal art through three case studies: language games and phonological structure in Chatino (Campbell 2020), tonal textsetting in Tlahuapa Tù'un Sàví (Sleeper and Basurto 2022), and tonal analysis and the Sambla balafon surrogate language (McPherson 2018b, 2019b). We then turn to the implications of music and the verbal arts for phonological theory.

4.1 Case Studies

Language games, also known as ludlings, are a form of language play that alter the phonological structure of words in a systematic way, "for the purposes of concealment or comic effect" (Laycock 1972: 61). Indeed, given the systematicity of the alterations, Bagemihl (1988) considers language games (as well as musical surrogate languages, to be covered shortly) as "alternative phonologies." Campbell (2020) discusses a language game known as *ñʃ-akwiʔ t͡sūʔ ntīlú* 'speaking backwards' in Zenzontepec Chatino, an Otomanguean language spoken in Oaxaca State, Mexico. At the time of documentation, the language game had already fallen into disuse after its inventor moved away in the mid-twentieth century, further underscoring the importance of documenting these often ephemeral genres of verbal art. In terms of methodology, the data are thus a combination of forms spontaneously offered by a speaker/rememberer of the play language and forms elicited by Campbell to probe the rules of the play language in different phonological contexts. This combination of naturalistic data with targeted elicitation is a common theme in phonological analysis in the context of language documentation, as the naturalistic data give rise to hypotheses that must then be tested across a range of contexts that may not present themselves in the naturally occurring forms. (Indeed, the same could be said for all levels of linguistic analysis.)

Based on these data, Campbell determined that the fundamental rule of *nīʔ-akwiʔ tsūʔ ntīlú* is to move the initial syllable of the word to the end of the word, such as *kʷela* -> *lákʷe* 'fish', *kutunu* -> *tūnúku* 'large crayfish'. As he notes, there is often a question of whether laryngealization in Zapotecan languages is a suprasegmental feature of the nucleus or the result of a medial glottal stop. In Zenzontepec Chatino, the play language provides evidence for a glottal stop, which becomes word initial after the original initial syllable is transposed to the end of the word, for example, *tʲáʔa* -> *ʔátʲa* 'relative of'. It similarly provides evidence that consonant clusters are complex onsets rather than being split into a coda and onset, as the consonants remain together after the initial syllable is transposed, as in *kíʔju* -> *ʔjúki* 'male'. Results like these demonstrate how the study of language games can provide a source of evidence for phonological analysis; for further discussion, see Campbell (2020).

A second example of marrying phonological analysis with documentation of verbal arts comes from another Otomanguean language, Tlahuapa Tù'un Sàví (Mixtecan). Sleeper and Basurto (2022) describe their methodology for studying how the language's tones are set to melodies in vocal music. Like other studies of tonal textsetting (e.g., Wong and Diehl 2002; Schellenberg 2012; Kirby and Ladd 2016; McPherson and Ryan 2018), the authors focus on the directionality of transitions from one tone to the next compared to the transitions between the musical notes they are set to. For instance, a sequence of H tone followed by M tone is descending, and if it is set to a descending sequence of notes, then the textsetting is said to be parallel. If it were instead set to a rising sequence of notes, then the textsetting is said to be opposing. If either tone or melody is level, coupled with rising or falling, then the textsetting is said to be oblique, which together with parallel mappings forms the category "non-opposing." In addition to studying tonal textsetting in Tlahuapa Tù-un Sàví, the authors developed a workflow for incorporating melodic information in ABC notation (Walshaw 2011) into ELAN transcriptions (Brugman and Russel 2004); these transcriptions can then be imported into musical notation software like MuseScore to produce Western musical staff notation or to convert it into another musical notation system.[22]

Sleeper and Basurto found that tonal textsetting in Tlahuapa Tù'un Sàví is toward the stricter end of the cross-linguistic textsetting spectrum, with 88 percent parallel mappings and 99 percent non-opposing. Some of the few cases of mismatch between tone and tune could be explained by looking to the phonology,

---

[22] Of course, not every musical tradition conforms to Western musical conventions. Sleeper and Basurto (2022) note that there are extensions to ABC notation to take into account microtonal variations used in, for instance, Middle Eastern music, but whether or not even modified Western musical notation ought to be used for non-Western music remains up for debate.

specifically at tone sandhi. The authors note that Tlahuapa Tù'un Sàví may have a tone sandhi process of upstep, where when two H tones meet across a word boundary, the second is pronounced on a higher pitch. This process may be reflected in tonal textsetting, allowing a sequence of two H tones to be sung on a rising melody without this constituting an oblique or non-parallel mapping. Thus, once again, we see a symbiotic relationship between the study of a language's phonology and the documentation of its verbal arts: Phonological analysis lays the groundwork for understanding the artistic adaptation of language, while musical or poetic details in the verbal art form can in return shed light on phonemic distinctions or phonological processes. Sleeper and Basurto further suggest that textsetting may offer insights into the phonemic status of vowel length in Tlahuapa Tù'un Sàví, though they leave the question for future work.

The final example, drawn from the second author's own experience (McPherson 2018b, 2019b), comes from the realm of music. In the documentation of Seenku (Mande; Burkina Faso), McPherson wanted to include music in the corpus and asked her main consultants if they had any examples they could share. Expecting vocal music (as this was *language* documentation, after all), she was surprised and admittedly a little disappointed to be played recordings of seemingly instrumental music on the *balafon*, a resonator xylophone. However, one consultant quickly told her that he "knew what the balafon was saying." She unexpectedly found herself in the face of a musical surrogate language, a system that transforms linguistic content into musical form (McPherson 2018b; Winter and McPherson 2022). She worked with balafon musicians, including Mamadou Diabate, the internationally renowned musician whose music was brought to her in the first place, to decipher the system. As Campbell did with the Chatino language game, this involved transcribing and analyzing both naturally occurring phrases in the music (e.g., common requests for money) and also eliciting novel phrases to explore a full range of phonological contrasts and contexts, as well as the productivity of the surrogate system. It quickly became apparent that the surrogate language encodes the tone and rhythm of Seenku words without any reference to segmental identity (McPherson 2018b).

Just as the Chatino ludling provided evidence for syllable structure and other phonological questions, so too did the balafon surrogate language provide a crucial source of evidence in Seenku tonal analysis (McPherson 2019b). At the time when the author began working on the balafon surrogate language, she was still in the midst of analyzing Seenku's tone system. It was clearly complex, with multiple contour tones, but the number of contrastive levels was yet to be determined – only three seemed to be required for the citation forms of nouns and verbs, but a fourth level would appear in some morphosyntactic and phonological contexts, as well as in some closed-class vocabulary like numerals or proper names.[23] Balafon musicians are highly attuned to the tone system and seemed to faithfully encode each tonal component, including all tones in a contour tone (e.g., a HX-toned word like *bî* 'goat' would be played with a quick succession of the note encoding H followed by the note encoding X, i.e., Extra-low), and so she was eager to hear how they would encode these mystery tonal forms. Here she found a very consistent fourth tone level, which she eventually called Low (in contrast with Extra-low), that explained all of these forms: Singular X-toned nouns raised one step higher in plural formation (*bè̤ɛ* -> *bɛ̀ɛ* 'pig(s)', McPherson 2017a); proper names and a small handful of other closed-class vocabulary like *nɔ̀* 'five' were played on this fourth level; and certain auxiliaries that appeared to alternate between (in a three-tone analysis) High, downstepped High, Low, and this intermediate level were always played as a rising tone from what is now called Low to what is now called Super-high. In other words, the balafon represents the underlying form of the contour tone rather than its surface forms after contour tone simplification. Thanks to this unique source of evidence – a musical surrogate language – the remaining mysteries in Seenku's tone system were resolved, all while documenting a rich and culturally important musico-linguistic tradition. See McPherson (2019b) for more detailed discussion and exemplification.

4.2 Theoretical Implications

The verbal arts have enjoyed a long relationship with phonological theory. This is especially true for metrical poetry, where the field of generative metrics has yielded important insights into prosodic structure and syllable weight (Halle and Keyser 1966, 1971; Kiparsky 1975, 1977; Hayes 1989; Ryan 2011, 2014, to name but a few); for a recent overview, see Blumenfeld (2016). Much of this work is based on classical languages (Greek, Latin, Arabic, etc.), where large written corpora facilitate quantitative analysis. But more recent work in language documentation has adapted this methodology to a more diverse range of languages. For example, Hayes and Schuh (2019) use Maximum Entropy Harmonic Grammar (Goldwater and Johnson 2003; Hayes et al. 2012) to model the metrics and musical textsetting of the *rajaz* meter in Hausa (Chadic, Nigeria). Like many of the classical meters, *rajaz* is quantity sensitive, with heavy syllables including both CVC and CVV. There is moraic equivalence in certain positions in the metra (lines), whereby two light syllables are treated as the equivalent of one heavy syllable. The authors show, however, that metrically prominent positions in the line attract heavy syllables; the higher the prominence, the greater the proportion

---

[23] This further underscores the point from Section 2 that different lexical classes can show different phonological behavior, which lexicography can help uncover.

of heavy syllables. Metrical bracketing is also sensitive to the prosodic hierarchy (see also Hayes 1989), with line breaks generally aligned with phonological phrase breaks and an avoidance of word boundaries inside poetic feet. Data from other languages and metrical styles can thus reinforce (or potentially challenge) established models of metrical organization and the phonological structure on which they are based.

Like many in non-Western traditions, there is no division in Hausa between poetry and music: *Rajaz* poetry is standardly sung, but interestingly, the musical rhythms used for *rajaz* are distinct from the metrical rhythms of the poetry. Hayes and Schuh (2019) consider a number of hypotheses on the relationship between metrical grids and musical grids in generating *rajaz* poetry (as the texts are improvised), but ultimately leave the question open. Instead, they delve deeper into the phonetic realization of the sung texts by developing a quantitative model of phonetic duration, following work by Flemming (2001), Katz (2010), Ryan (2011), Lefkowitz (2017), and others. Hayes and Schuh's constraint-based analysis models the durational compromise between phonological targets – the syllable and the mora – and musical targets. One interesting result is that in sung verse, the ratio of syllable to mora comes somewhat closer to the idealized ratio of 2:1 than in prose, as the musical grid stretches syllables out further than they would be in regular speech.

Fitting language to metrical grids, whether quantity sensitive or insensitive, can involve morphophonological strategies not otherwise seen in the regular grammar of the language. For example, in Blackfoot (Algonquian; Canada and the United States) lullabies, Miyashita (2011) reports a partial reduplication pattern to add a syllable; unlike in Tohono O'odham (Uto-Aztecan; Mexico and the United States), where a meaningful reduplication pattern is co-opted without its usual meaning to fit a metrical grid (Fitzgerald 1998), regular Blackfoot grammar has no reduplication, and yet speakers can still draw on this common cross-linguistic phonological process when a need arises. In Nanti (Arawakan; Peru), the *karintaa* verse genre involves seven-mora lines, and partial reduplication can likewise be used to stretch out a line that would otherwise be too short (Michael 2019). Interestingly, though, if the line is too long, truncation is also found. Unlike reduplication, this is a typologically rare morphophonological process (see Weeda 1992 for discussion), yet it too can arise in the domain of the verbal arts. In both Blackfoot and Nanti, vocables (meaningless poetic syllables) can also be inserted, with their distribution sensitive to prosodic structure.

Poetry and the music–language interface ultimately shed light on speakers' metalinguistic knowledge of their phonology. In order to manipulate phonological structures, one must be aware of them, either consciously or subconsciously. When phonological structure is adapted differently in different genres, it can point to psychologically real distinctions between different levels of structure. McPherson (2019b) makes such an argument for the distinction between lexical and postlexical tonal processes in Seenku (Mande; Burkina Faso). The Sambla balafon surrogate language, discussed in Section 4.1, encodes all lexical and grammatical tone processes but eschews postlexical processes like contour tone simplification. However, tonal textsetting of vocal music does encode the postlexical level of tone (McPherson and James 2021), showing that both levels of phonological structure are available for artistic adaptation but that the distinction between lexical and postlexical phonology is psychologically real in a way that would be difficult to argue from spoken language alone.

5 Grammar Writing

Descriptive grammars have been and continue to be one of the main sources of our understanding of language structures cross-linguistically and form an important source of inquiry for linguistic typology and theory. As comprehensive treatments of individual linguistic systems, grammars also provide an invaluable resource for speech communities seeking to revitalize and reclaim their languages in cases of severe language obsolescence or language shift. Much has been written in the literature about the desiderata in grammar writing (see, for instance, the articles in Payne & Weber 2007, Ameka et al. 2006, and Nakayama & Rice 2014). The role of sound systems and their analysis in the context of grammatical descriptions has, however, been generally neglected in the literature (cf. Rice 2014). In this section, we address challenges and opportunities for phonological analysis within the context of *documentation-based* grammar writing (as a different enterprise than that of grammar writing within the traditional canon of Americanist linguistics). We also discuss the properties that grammatical descriptions should ideally have in terms of phonological description and analysis, both for a better understanding of linguistic systems as a whole, as well as for a better understanding of individual phonological systems. In Section 6 we address how this holistic approach to phonological analysis and grammatical description has important ramifications for language pedagogy in the context of language revitalization and reclamation. Throughout the section, we will draw on our experiences as phonologist-grammarians.

Before addressing the relationship between phonology and grammar writing, we discuss what we assume to be involved in grammar writing within the context of language documentation. We turn to this next.

5.1 Documentation-Based Grammar Writing

As we have described, grammatical descriptions seek to provide a coherent treatment of the structures, patterns, and phenomena of a language variety and how they interact within the larger context of the language as a whole (Evans and Dench 2006).[24] They are designed to provide a comprehensive description and analysis of a language in each language's own terms, carefully developing the language-internal criteria and evidence that motivate postulating the grammatical categories identified (Cristofaro 2006). At the same time, grammatical descriptions often also seek to identify the ways in which the particular language variety described resembles other languages (both related and unrelated), situating the analysis of phenomena and patterns in the grammar within the context of relevant typological and theoretical literature.

The grammar-writing process in the Boasian tradition involves a close reliance on a corpus of texts, with grammatical structures and patterns often being illustrated with data examples drawn from the associated text collection in the finished product. In the framework of language documentation, however, the process of grammar writing involves an even closer interaction between the development of the text corpus and data analysis for grammatical description, enabled both by the digital nature of contemporary language corpora and the expanded range of genres that is typical in language documentation, as discussed in Section 3. This closer interaction has specific implications for the process of grammar writing. First, the digital nature of the documentary corpus allows the analyst to access multimedia recordings (which are ideally high quality) and easily find examples of specific constructions and patterns in different contexts.[25] This in turn allows the grammatical description to be enhanced with an assessment of the distribution of specific patterns and constructions, providing statements of their frequency within the corpus.

Second, the digital corpus also allows the possibility of supplementing specific data examples with corresponding audio or video recordings, as well as links to the specific texts from which the examples were drawn; this makes the grammatical description *reproducible*, as defined and exemplified in Section 3: Grammar readers may access the primary materials from which the grammatical description is based upon and will be able to verify whether the

---

[24] This system-wide dimension is what Sapir refers to as the 'genius' of a language: "[T]here is such a thing as a basic plan, a certain cut, to each language. This type or plan or structural 'genius' of the language is something much more fundamental, much more pervasive, than any single feature of it that we can mention, nor can we gain an adequate idea of its nature by a mere recital of the sundry facts that make up the grammar of the language" (Sapir 1921: 172).

[25] An anonymous reviewer brings up an important point, namely that high-quality recordings of speech are not possible in all situations, and that the quality of recordings may be suitable or not for different purposes, including recordings for fine phonetic analysis.

analyses and descriptions provided in the grammar are sound. Embedding sound from the documentary corpus into examples in grammar writing is also significantly valuable for members of the speech community who are interested in accessing the grammatical description for community-centered language planning (see also discussion in Rice 2014 and in Section 6).

Finally, the expanded range of genres of the documentary corpus allows us to more centrally incorporate patterns of variation into grammatical description. Specifically, and as noted by Mosel (2014: 136), there are at least three kinds of variation that can be incorporated into grammatical description: "the grammatical variation in spontaneous oral texts and the edited versions of these texts; the preference for certain grammatical constructions in particular text varieties; and the pervasive use of certain constructions in texts on special themes".

5.2 Phonological Analysis and Documentation-Based Grammar Writing

As with lexicography, discussed in Section 2, and indeed language documentation as a whole, phonology and grammar writing are in a symbiotic relationship. In this subsection, we consider the ways in which writing a documentation-based grammar enhances our understanding of the phonological system of a language; in Section 5.3, we flip this relationship and consider what working on the phonology of a language brings to the process of grammar writing.

As discussed earlier, the goal of grammar writing is to produce a comprehensive description of a language's grammatical system. Phonology, of course, operates at every level of the grammar, from individual words to entire complex utterances. Nevertheless, canonical phonological analysis often considers constituents at the smaller end of the spectrum: stem- and word-level phonology, morphophonological alternations, and perhaps local sandhi effects. When writing a grammar, the phonologist is necessarily confronted with much larger constituents, making it much more likely to uncover phonological patterns at the interface with morphosyntax as well as postlexical phonology.

We illustrate the point here with a case of grammatical tone in Seenku (Mande; Burkina Faso) from the second author's work. Seenku displays the prototypical Mande word order of Subject Auxiliary Object Verb X, where X can be an adverb, postpositional phrase, or other adjunct. Between the subject and the auxiliary, we find a number of enclitics marking tense and mood. (Aspect, on the other hand, is typically encoded through grammatical tone on the verb stem.) There is variation in whether the clitics are realized segmentally or whether they consist only of tone and a mora concatenated with the subject. For instance, the past-tense clitic *lē* with Super-high (S) tone can also be realized simply as the addition of an S-toned mora to the end of the subject's tone, as in *mó lě* vs. *móǒ* '1sg pst'. The text corpus reveals that the segmental form is rare; in naturalistic speech, these are almost always suprasegmentally marked through tone and lengthening.

This past-tense marker was identified early on in working on Seenku, as it appears in a relatively basic construction targeted early even in elicitation. Other post-subject clitics – or often their tonal effects – were only found much later as the combination of text transcription and grammar writing revealed more complex syntactic constructions. Consider, for example, the subjunctive enclitic *lé* with High (H) tone. (Interestingly, almost all of these post-subject enclitics have the segmental content *le*, making an understanding of the tone system and its inclusion at every level of the grammar that much more crucial, a point we return to in Section 5.3.) One environment where this enclitic is found is in conditional clauses, a construction unlikely to be targeted by a phonologist outside of the context of grammatical description. It is likewise found in some complement clauses, such as in the complement of the verbal construction 'want' (i.e., "I want that you-SBJV do . . . "). Yet another enclitic *lě* which can (and often does) leave only its tone behind is the subordinating *lě* found after the subject of relative clauses and in some temporally subordinated clauses.

Again, it is often text collection and transcription that first reveals these constructions; writing a grammar forces the linguist to probe them further, testing hypotheses about their structure with elicitation and comparison with other examples in the text corpus. In Seenku, tone acts as a sort of "grammatical glue," with often subtle (to the non-native speaker's ear) contour tones indicating the syntactic structure of the clause and the grammatical role played by the subject. Further, from a purely phonological standpoint, these grammatical tone patterns reveal possible contour tones not found at the lexical level. Lexically, Seenku displays HS and LS rising tones, HX falling tones, and XHX bell-shaped tones (rise–fall). These three grammatical particles alone add three more rising tones (XS, XH, and LH), three more falling tones (SX, LX, and SH), and numerous other three-tone contours (e.g., HXS, HXH) to the inventory of possible, albeit derived, contour tones. Without describing the grammar more holistically, these contour tones may never have been identified, yielding an incomplete view of Seenku's phonology.

5.3 The Role of Phonology in Comprehensive Grammatical Descriptions

We now turn to the question of the ways in which analyzing a phonological system contributes to the process of grammar writing. As we claim in this subsection, a detailed analysis of the phonological system of a language is essential for understanding other grammatical domains and the language as a whole, as phonology permeates phenomena, patterns, and constructions at every structural level of a linguistic system.

An overview of what has historically been included in terms of sound in reference grammars is found in Rice (2014). The focus in this overview is on grammars of North American languages produced during the twentieth century and within the Americanist tradition. For the grammars surveyed, Rice finds that the chapter on phonology generally includes a description of phonemic inventories, allophonic processes, syllable structure, distributional constraints on sound patterns, and morphophonological phenomena, as well as discussion of prosodic characteristics and processes. In this tradition, there is already a precedent for discussion of patterns of variation and of different speech styles (see Section 3), but a strong emphasis is placed on the analysis of word-level phonological phenomena, with phonological phenomena above the word level generally absent from grammatical descriptions. Crucially, this tradition seems to be permeated by an implicit assumption that the phonological description and the treatment of the morphology, syntax, and semantics of a language are separate tasks, with little interaction between the phonological component and other grammatical domains. Moreover, a greater emphasis is placed on developing the morphological and syntactic descriptions of grammars, with limited attention to phonological phenomena.

As discussed in Rice (2014), more recent grammars show changes that reflect the technological developments that are also crucial in language documentation as a field in its own right. The ability to produce high-quality recordings has several implications for the description of phonological systems in reference grammars. One immediate consequence is the ability to gather instrumental data of sound systems. An increasing number of grammatical descriptions include phonetic illustrations (e.g., spectrograms, waveforms, formant plots) of particularly interesting or typologically unusual phonetic and phonological structures. Some recent examples include the grammars of Kalamang (Papuan; Indonesia) (Visser 2022), Gyeli (Bantu A801; Cameroon) (Grimm 2021), and Choguita Rarámuri (Uto-Aztecan; Mexico) (Caballero 2022a), to name only a few.[26] More recent grammatical descriptions are also increasingly addressing the phonology of higher levels of prosodic structure. Some examples include Movima (isolate; Bolivia) (Haude 2006), Dolakha Newar (Tibeto-Burman;

---

[26] As Rice (2014: 75) notes, some earlier grammatical descriptions sought to visually represent the acoustic realization of sound patterns in grammatical descriptions, as exemplified in Sapir's (1912) grammar of Takelma (isolate; US), where musical notation is used to illustrate the phonetic realization of tonal patterns in the language.

Phonology in Language Documentation

Nepal) (Genetti 2007; cited in Rice 2014), Muskogee (Muskogean; United States) (Martin 2011), and Seenku (Mande; Burkina Faso) (McPherson 2020).

Beyond the expansion of what is included in the description of phonological systems, another important development in grammar writing is the increasing integration of the study of phonology and the study of morphology, syntax, and discourse structure. An example of this is found in Remijsen and Ayoker (2021), who describe the noun phrase structure of Shilluk (Nilotic; Sudan) as part of the grammatical description of the language based on a corpus of spontaneous speech and targeted elicitation. Of interest here is the discussion of phonological criteria, including reduction processes and tonal interactions between stems and clitics, for diagnosing patterns of cliticization in noun phrases containing deictic markers. In this chapter, Remijsen and Ayoker (2021: 70) also provide an analysis of complex patterns of exponence of the vocative, which is marked at the right edge of the nominal phrase and involves a tone pattern that interacts with the morphological properties and lexical phonological specification of the base morpheme (namely, the presence/absence of floating quantity).[27] The phonological evidence supplements the morphosyntactic arguments for the claims presented, and representative examples drawn both from the corpus and elicitation are provided with embedded audio files.

Finally, a relevant question with respect to phonology and grammar writing concerns how to organize the grammatical description itself. From the perspective we adopt here, a comprehensive grammatical description and analysis of any language is incomplete if the complex interactions between its phonology and other grammatical domains is not addressed. As discussed in Mosel (2006), while most grammars have an ascending macrostructure (phonology > morphology > syntax, etc.), this structure has its limits when complex interactions between patterns across different levels of the grammar must be addressed. Traditionally, these interactions are captured through cross-references in grammatical descriptions. For instance, typologists interested in the phonology–syntax interface would rely on a robust cross-reference system in order to discover whether a particular language exhibits relevant patterns.

An alternative is to have dedicated chapters in grammatical descriptions for complex interactions, in addition to cross-references between chapters. An example is found in Martin's (2011) grammar of Muskogee (Muskogean;

---

[27] Rice (2014) discusses further examples of grammatical descriptions where phonological evidence plays a role in the description and analysis of other domains of the grammar. An example she cites is that of Aikhenvald's (2003) grammar of Tariana (Arawak; Brazil), which discusses the phonological properties of phrasing beyond the level of the phonological word. Another example cited in Rice (2014) is Genetti's (2007) grammar of Dolakha Newar (Tibeto-Burman; Nepal), where detailed discussion of the relationship between prosodic and syntactic structuring is provided.

USA): In addition to individual chapters on the phonemic inventory, general phonological processes, stress, tone and intonation, segmental phonology, syllabic structure, and other word-level suprasegmental processes, a dedicated chapter addresses phonological structures and patterns in terms of their organization in higher prosodic units and/or across grammatical domains. Another example is the first author's grammar of Choguita Rarámuri (Caballero 2022a). As discussed in Section 3, this language is prosodically complex, featuring a "hybrid" word prosodic system with both stress and tone in its lexical phonology, grammatical tone patterns, and tonal and non-tonal encoding of intonation. These patterns are analyzed in dedicated chapters for stress, tone and intonation, nominal morphology, verb morphology, and sentence types (where intonation patterns associated with interrogative and imperative constructions are described). A chapter, "Prosody: Domains and interactions," provides readers with an overview of structures and processes that crosscut the grammar of the language with the goal of addressing how the principles applying in different grammatical domains yield surface forms in the language.

In sum, we propose that a detailed, careful description and analysis of a language's phonological system is essential in understanding other grammatical domains of a language and their complex interrelationships in the context of a grammatical description that seeks to be comprehensive. As Rice (2014: 80) observes, "[p]honology is definitely a level that interrelates continuously with all other levels, and to study the other areas without reference to sound has become increasingly unacceptable as the methods have allowed for this study."

6 Phonological Documentation and Community Goals

As mentioned in Section 1, one important development in the field of language documentation is a changing engagement with Indigenous language communities and scholarship that examines broader ethical issues (e.g., Grinevald 2003; Czaykowska-Higgins 2009, 2018; Holton 2009; Rice 2010, 2011a, 2011b; Good 2018; Holton et al. 2022). In this changing context, the perspectives, priorities, and goals of language communities are central in the planning of language documentation, not only for the purpose of better supporting language community needs but also for improvement of the scientific value of language documentation (see the discussion in Leonard 2018). In this section, we discuss the implications of this changing paradigm for the field of phonology.

We begin our discussion with an example of the San Juan Piñas Mixtec language project described in Section 1.4. As described there, this project focuses on the documentation and analysis of the San Juan Piñas Mixtec language, where the goals and priorities of community members are central in shaping the methods and outcomes of the project. While San Juan Piñas Mixtec is used in daily interactions in the town of San Juan Piñas and many elderly speakers are monolingual, younger speakers are bilingual in San Juan Piñas Mixtec and Spanish. In diaspora communities in California, younger San Juan Piñas Mixtec speakers tend to be passive bilinguals, with English and/or Spanish as their dominant language(s). With continued migration of speakers from Oaxaca to diaspora communities, there is a trend of increasing language attrition and language shift. Given the vulnerability of intergenerational transmission of the language, Claudia Juárez Chávez and other San Juan Piñas Mixtec language experts are interested in the development of language resources designed for the promotion and revitalization of the language on both sides of the border, including: (i) lexical resources for a trilingual talking dictionary for Android app and web page use (Juárez Chávez et al. 2022);[28] (ii) video recordings of cultural and ecological documentation in San Juan Piñas with trilingual subtitles; and (iii) creative works in San Juan Piñas Mixtec with Spanish and English translations to distribute in the town of San Juan Piñas in printed form, among other materials. Given that these resources include the orthographic representation of the language, Claudia Juárez Chávez was specially interested in using the developing tonal analysis of San Juan Piñas Mixtec for informing how to represent tone patterns orthographically, given the complexity of the tone system in this language variety. Specifically, the San Juan Piñas Mixtec tonal system involves a close interaction between lexical tone and grammatical tone, plus a number of register effects which yield six phonetic tone levels from various phonetic, phonological, and morphological sources (Duarte Borquez et al. in press).[29]

Given this complexity of surface tonal patterns, language experts faced decisions as to what to represent in the spelling of the language. Claudia Juárez Chávez opted for a maximally informative representation of tone, encoding both lexical and grammatical tones, and where each tone is encoded on a single vowel using diacritics, in order to disambiguate tonal contours on single morae that may encode both grammatical and lexical contrasts, among other properties of the tone system. For instance, some words have rising contours in

---

[28] The San Juan Piñas Mixtec talking dictionary is modeled after the talking dictionaries developed for Zapotec languages described in Harrison et al. (2019).

[29] The phonological analysis of the San Juan Piñas Mixtec tone system can be summarized as follows: (i) Lexical tone specifications are based on three tone primitives (H, L, and M); (ii) lexical and post-lexical tonal processes derive phonetic tone targets from lexical specifications; (iii) there is a contrast between underlyingly specified M tones and underlyingly toneless TBUs that receive M tone by default or through tone spreading; (iv) morphemes may sponsor floating L tones; (v) tonal processes and distributions are constrained/operate in domains that are prosodic and/or morphological in nature; (vi) morphosyntactically triggered melodies concatenate with or replace lexical tones; (vii) the surface tone patterns in inflected words are determined by phonological and morphosyntactic factors (for further discussion, see Caballero et al. in press).

single morae as part of their lexical tone specification, for example, the LM contour in /ti^{13}na^{3+1}/ 'dog,' represented orthographically as <tīīnā>, while other words have rising contours in single morae encoding inflectional values, for example, the past and irrealis negative polarity forms of the verbal lexeme /^{n}di^{3}ko^3/ 'grind,' with an LM contour in the past form /^{n}di^{13}ko^3/ 'ground' and an LH contour in the negative irrealis form /^{n}di^{15}ko^3/ 'will not grind,' spelled as <ndǐīkō> and <ndǐíkō>, respectively. This stands in contrast to the orthographic representations available for other Mixtec language varieties, where only tones with grammatical functions are represented in order to facilitate the literacy process (Snider 2018, citing personal communication from Inga McKendry).[30] In the case of San Juan Piñas Mixtec, a maximally informative spelling convention of tone aims to support the acquisition of complex tonal patterns for a new generation of San Juan Piñas Mixtec speakers who may only have passive knowledge of the language or no fluency at all. Furthermore, this spelling convention reflects the current phonological analysis of the language, which reveals that the interaction between lexical and grammatical tones, while largely predictable phonologically, is complex enough that is difficult to separate lexical and grammatical tones in the orthographic representation (for more discussion, see Caballero et al. 2024). Crucially, while the phonological analysis was developed jointly by all team members, and the technical aspects of the analysis were instrumental in laying out different options for orthographic representation, the decision-making process was squarely within the hands of language experts co-leading the project. In this respect, this project follows the model established in other work that centers the needs and goals of community members in linguistic research (see, e.g., Czaykowska-Higgins 2009 and Rice 2011b) and in particular within the context of orthography development (Hinton 2014; Beier and Michael 2023; see also discussion in Cahill and Rice 2014).

We note that there has been a long-standing interest in the field of linguistics and allied fields about the complexities of representing spoken language in written form, especially within the context of Indigenous language communities (e.g., Fishman 1977; Sebba 2007; Cahill and Rice 2014). While this interest predates the establishment of the field of language documentation per se, it becomes central within an ethnographic approach to language documentation, as it concerns the political, ideological, and social realities of the speech communities intending to develop orthographies for their languages. One dimension of complexity in orthographic representation and potential implications for community dynamics is the question of how to handle variation. In the

---

[30] Other aspects of the orthographic representation developed for San Juan Piñas Mixtec are based on conventions developed for the *Ve'e Tu'un Savi* (Mixtec Language Academy), the Summer Institute of Linguistics (SIL), and Mexico's National Institute of Indigenous Languages (INALI in Spanish).

case of the San Juan Piñas Mixtec language project, language experts are especially concerned that the language be represented accurately and that language resources be designed with the flexibility to reflect inter- and intra-speaker variation. For instance, in the developing San Juan Piñas Mixtec talking dictionary, this includes representing variability in the realization of allophonic processes (such as pre-aspiration of voiceless obstruents in certain prosodic positions or implementation of tonal upstep). This is accomplished through IPA transcriptions and accompanying audio clips, which are included in order to illustrate the details of surface individual productions; for example, the adjective stem /i⁵tʃi⁵/ 'dry' is represented orthographically as <ichi> (a phonemic representation) but phonetically in IPA as [i⁵ʰtʃi⁶], with phonetic representation of both pre-aspiration and upstep of the second H tone, to match the audio clip of this particular entry. Furthermore, when individual lexical items have different realizations for different speakers, each phonological realization of these lexical items is given a separate entry with their corresponding spelling reflecting the differences.

This approach to representing variation stems from a concern that the spelling used in the language resources produced through the project should not be considered a standard orthography; instead, the goal is to accommodate additional spelling preferences that other speakers may have and that may emerge during the course of the project. The current design thus reflects the design used for the development of talking dictionaries for Zapotec languages, where single entries may have multiple spellings and where there may be multiple entries for a single lexeme. The incorporation of audio or other multimedia supports the flexibility in orthographic representation or the lack of an orthographic representation entirely (Harrison et al. 2019). This design tries to minimize the potential negative ramifications that may arise of inadvertently imposing a standard orthography (see Leonard 2018 and Beier & Michael 2023 for discussion).

Finally, one other important way in which phonological documentation and community goals intersect is in the implementation of methodologies that incorporate language teaching and linguistic training of members of speech communities. An example of this is illustrated in the work of the Chatino project at UT Austin in the study of tonal phenomena of Chatino languages (Otomanguean; Mexico). As Cruz and Woodbury (2014) state:

> We ... emphasize the continued role [in working out the tone system] of teaching and speaker-training in local contexts. This has been possible ... because of the high levels of interest and appreciation of Chatino in Chatino communities, and the view that writing is a way for the language to receive respect. ... [R]esearch can be more exact when speakers, through linguistic

study and through learning to write, become critically aware of the tonological systems of their languages. (Cruz & Woodbury 2014: 521; cited in Seifart et al. 2018: e329)

In sum, centering perspectives, concerns, and goals from language communities is not only a way to advance our field's ethical practices, but also a way of advancing the methodologies and analyses of sound systems and other levels of linguistic structure of underdocumented languages.

7 Conclusion

In this Element, we have illustrated the symbiotic relationship that exists between language documentation and theoretical phonology and phonological analysis. Each field is enriched by the other in terms of data, methodologies, and guiding questions. Of course, language documentation as a field is meant to be multipurpose, serving the needs of language communities, linguists of different stripes, and scholars in fields beyond the language sciences such as anthropologists, musicologists, or historians, among others. As such, the language documentarian must wear multiple hats to keep in mind all of these potential uses of the materials. From the point of view of phonological theory and analysis, we note simply that high-quality audiovisual materials, careful transcriptions, and detailed metadata are of utmost importance. Where possible, the language documentarian should remain sensitive to patterns of variation, both within and across speakers, and annotate these patterns in some way.

We would also like to end this Element by encouraging phonologists to get involved in language documentation. There may be a perception that language documentation is the domain of morphosyntacticians (working on typology and formal theory), but phonologists bring an important skill set to the field, as any successful language documentation project is grounded in careful phonemic analysis and transcription. Language documentation guided by phonological questions will produce a diverse text corpus, including different genres (such as the verbal arts), different speech rates and styles, and different speakers. As phonology plays a crucial role across multiple levels of grammar, close attention paid to phonological patterns, including tone, intonation, and phrasing, can deepen our understanding of the grammatical system as a whole.

Looking to the future, advances in computational tools may help streamline the process of data transcription, which could yield larger and more diverse corpora for both documentary and phonological purposes. Transcription is a well-known bottleneck in language documentation (Seifart et al. 2018), where it can take hours to produce a detailed transcription of just a minute or two of speech. The past decade has seen a dramatic increase in work on automatic speech recognition (ASR) and other machine-learning tools for under-resourced languages (e.g., Adams et al. 2019; Prud'hommeaux et al. 2021; Coto Solano et al. 2022). The larger corpora these tools could help produce would allow phonologists to further expand stochastic methods and quantitative analysis to a more diverse range of languages; conversely, a better phonological understanding of both contextual and sociolinguistic variation can help fine-tune these computational models, which often struggle with dialectal variation even in high-resource languages (e.g., Nigmatulina et al. 2020; Wassink et al. 2022; Besdouri et al. 2024).

These developments bring enormous advantages with respect to the accessibility of documentary materials for different audiences and for a variety of agendas. This crucially includes benefits for Indigenous language communities that seek to leverage the internet and other digital technologies in order to establish a digital presence for their languages and as a means to promote and revitalize their languages and cultures (see, for instance, projects focused on NLP developments for Indigenous Languages of the Americas [https://turing.iimas.unam.mx/americasnlp/] and digital initiatives for language activism, as in the case of the project Rising Voices [https://rising.globalvoices.org/]).

At the same time, alongside the development of computational and other tools that allow the processing of large amounts of linguistic data in corpora for multiple agendas, there is an urgent need to consider potential implications that the uses of these data may bring to Indigenous speech communities. For widely spoken languages represented in "Big Data," Holton et al. (2022) note that "[e]thical protocols in these contexts are driven by commercial interests in legal frameworks divorced from the cultural values or political realities and concerns of Indigenous communities." In this context, the questions of ownership, access, and control of linguistic (and other) data about Indigenous peoples is central to the Indigenous Data Sovereignty (IDS) movement, which "advocates for the direct involvement of Indigenous stakeholders in the collection, management, and use of data about Indigenous peoples" (Holton et al. 2022; see also Rainie et al. 2019). This includes phonological data, whether developed in documentary projects or accessed through archival materials, which in many cases are of central importance in efforts of language revitalization and reclamation. We thus encourage scholars working at the intersection of language documentation and phonology to consider these ethical protocols as central to their endeavors.

References

Adams, O., Cohn, T., Neubig, G., Cruz, H., Bird, S. & Michaud, A. (2019). Evaluating phonemic transcription of low-resource tonal languages for language documentation. In H. Isahara, B. Maegaard, S. Piperidis, C. Cieri, T. Declerck, K. Hasida, H. Mazo, K. Choukri, S. Goggi, J. Mariani, A. Moreno, N. Calzolari, J. Odijk and T. Tokunaga, eds., *11th International Conference on Language Resources and Evaluation, LREC 2018*. European Language Resources Association (ELRA), pp. 3356–3365.

Agodio, O., Bodji, S., Emil, S., Russell, K. & Sande, H. *Guébie Fieldwork Collection, 2014–15*. California Language Archive, Survey of California and Other Indian Languages. Berkeley, CA: University of California, Berkeley. http://dx.doi.org/doi:10.7297/X208639V.

Agostinho, A. L. & Antunes de Araujo, G. (2021). Playing with language: Three language games in the Gulf of Guinea. *Language Documentation and Conservation*, 15, 219–238.

Aguilar, A., Caballero, C., Carroll, L. & Garellek, M. (2015). Multidimensionality in the tonal realization of Choguita Rarámuri (Tarahumara). Talk presented at the 2015 Meeting of the Society for the Study of the Indigenous Languages of the Americas, Portland, Oregon, January 8–11, 2015.

Aikhenvald, A. (2003). *A Grammar of Tariana*. Cambridge Grammatical Descriptions. Cambridge, UK: Cambridge University Press.

Albright, A. (2002). Islands of reliability for regular morphology: Evidence from Italian. *Language*, 78, 684–709.

Ameka, F. K., Dench, A. & Evans, N. (eds.). (2006). *Catching Language: The Standing Challenge of Grammar Writing*. Berlin: De Gruyter Mouton.

Amith, J. (2020). Endangered language documentation: The challenges of interdisciplinary research in ethnobiology. In S. D. Penfield, ed., *Language Documentation & Conservation Special Publication No. 21: Interdisciplinary Approaches to Language Documentation*. Honolulu, HI: University of Hawai'I Press, pp. 72–112.

Anttila, A. (2002). Morphologically conditioned phonological alternations. *Natural Language & Linguistic Theory*, 20(1), 1–42.

Badenoch, N. (2019). The ethnopoetics of Sida animal names. 研究年報 [Journal of Research Institute], 60, 39–73.

Baese-Berk, M. & Goldrick, M. (2009). Mechanisms of interaction in speech production. *Language and Cognitive Processes*, 24(4), 527–554.

Bagemihl, B. (1988). Alternate phonologies and morphologies. PhD dissertation, University of British Columbia.

Baković, E. (2000). Harmony, dominance and control. PhD dissertation, Rutgers University.

Baksh-Comeau, Y. & Winer, L. (2016). Grasping the nettle: Handling flora entries in dictionaries. *Dictionaries: Journal of the Dictionary Society of North America*, 37(1), 36–59.

Becker, M. (2009). Phonological trends in the lexicon: The role of constraints. PhD dissertation, University of Massachusetts Amherst.

Beier, C. & Michael, L. (2023). Community-participatory orthography development in the Máíjùnà communities of Peruvian Amazonia. In D. Kavitskaya & A. C. L. Yu, eds., *The Life Cycle of Language: Past, Present and Future*. Oxford: Oxford University Press, pp. 291–314.

Bennett, R., Henderson, R. & Harvey, M. (2019). The interaction of tone and intonation in Uspanteko. In S. Calhoun, P. Escudero, M. Tabain & P. Warren, eds., *Proceedings of the International Congress of Phonetic Sciences (ICPhS) 2019*. Canberra: ASSTA, pp. 452–456.

Bennett, R., Henderson, R. & Harvey, M. (2022). Tonal variability and marginal contrast: Lexical pitch accent in Uspanteko. In H. Kubozono, J. Ito & A. Mester, eds., *Prosody and Prosodic Interfaces*. Oxford: Oxford University Press, pp. 187–226.

Berez-Kroeker, A. L., Gawne, L., Smythe Kung, S., Kelly, B. F., Heston, T., Holton, G., Pulsifer, P., Beaver, D. I., Chelliah, S., Dubinsky, S., Meier, R. P., Thieberger, N., Rice, K. & Woodbury, A. C. (2018). Reproducible research in linguistics: A position statement on data citation and attribution in our field. *Linguistics*, 56(1), 1–18.

Berko, J. (1958). The child's learning of English morphology. *Word*, 14(2–3), 150–177.

Besdouri, F. Z., Zribi, I. & Hadrich Belguith, L. (2024). Challenges and progress in developing speech recognition systems for Dialectal Arabic. *Speech Communication*, 163, 103110.

Bickford, J. A. & McKay-Cody, M. (2018). Endangerment and revitalization of sign languages. In L. Hinton, L. Huss & G. Roche, eds., *The Routledge Handbook of Language Revitalization*. New York: Routledge, pp. 255–264.

Blasi, D. E., Wichmann, S., Hammarström, H., Stadler, P. & Christiansen, M. (2016). Sound–meaning association biases evidenced across thousands of languages. *Proceedings of the National Academy of Sciences*, 113(39), 10818–10823.

Blumenfeld, L. (2016). Generative metrics: An overview. *Language and Linguistics Compass*, 10(9), 413–430.

References

Boas, F. (1911). Introduction. In F. Boas, ed., *Handbook of American Indian Languages* (vol. 1). Bureau of American Ethnology, Bulletin 40. Washington: Government Print Office, Smithsonian Institution, Bureau of American Ethnology, pp. 1–83.

Boersma, P. (1998). Functional phonology. PhD dissertation, University of Amsterdam.

Boersma, P. & Hayes, B. (2001). Empirical tests of the gradual learning algorithm. *Linguistic Inquiry*, 32(1), 45–86.

Boersma, P. & Pater, J. (2008/2016). Convergence properties of a gradual learning algorithm for Harmonic Grammar. In J. J. McCarthy & J. Pater, eds., *Harmonic Grammar and Harmonic Serialism*. Sheffield: Equinox, pp. 389–434. [Original electronic distribution 2008.]

Booij, G. (2000). The phonology–morphology interface. In L. Cheng & R. Sybesma, eds., The first Glot international state-of-the-article book. Berlin: de Gruyter, pp. 287–307.

Braconnier, C. (1982). *Le système tonal du dioula d'Odienné*. Abidjan: Université d'Abidjan.

Braconnier, C. & Diaby, S. (1982). *Dioula d'Odienné (parler de Samatiguila): matérial lexical*. Abidjan: Institut de Linguistique Appliquée.

Brown, R., Manmurulu, D., Manmurulu, J., O'Keeffe, I. & Singer, R. (2017). Maintaining song traditions and languages together at Warruwi (western Arnhem Land). In J. Wafer & M. Turpin, eds., *Recirculating Songs: Revitalising the Singing Practices of Indigenous Australia*. Sydney: Sydney University Press, pp. 268–285.

Brugman, H. & Russel, A. (2004). Annotating multimedia/multi-modal resources with ELAN. In M. T. Lino, M. F. Xavier, F. Ferreira, R. Costa & R. Silva, eds., *Proceedings of Fourth International Conference on Language Resources and Evaluation, Lisbon, 26–28 May*, pp. 2065–2068.

Brunelle, M. (2009). Tone perception in Northern and Southern Vietnamese. *Journal of Phonetics*, 37(1), 79–96.

Brunelle, M. (2012). Dialect experience and perceptual integrality in phonological registers: Fundamental frequency, voice quality and the first formant in Cham. *Journal of the Acoustical Society of America*, 131(4), 3088–3102.

Caballero, G. (2011). Morphologically conditioned stress assignment in Choguita Rarámuri (Tarahumara). *Linguistics*, 49(4), 749–790.

Caballero, G. (2015). *Choguita Rarámuri description and documentation*. Endangered Languages Archive. http://hdl.handle.net/2196/00-0000-0000-0001-86B4-0.

Caballero, G. (2022a). *A Grammar of Choguita Rarámuri: In Collaboration with Luz Elena León Ramírez, Sebastián Fuentes Holguín, Bertha Fuentes*

Loya and Other Choguita Rarámuri Language Experts. Berlin: Language Science Press.

Caballero, G. (2022b). Audio files accompanying the linguistic examples in "A grammar of Choguita Rarámuri." https://doi.org/10.5281/zenodo.7268366.

Caballero, G. & Carroll, L. (2015). Tone and stress in Choguita Rarámuri (Tarahumara) word prosody. *International Journal of American Linguistics*, 81(4), 457–493.

Caballero, G., Chai, Y. & Garellek, M. (2022). Stress, tone, and intonation in Choguita Rarámuri. In H. Kubozono, J. Ito & A. Mester, eds., *Prosody and Prosodic Interfaces*. Oxford: Oxford University Press, pp. 227–248.

Caballero, G., Duarte Borquez, C., Juárez Chávez, C. & Yuan, M. (in press). Lexical and grammatical tone in San Juan Piñas Mixtec (Tò'ōn Ndá'ví). *Phonological Data & Analysis*.

Caballero, G. & German, A. (2021). Grammatical tone patterns in Choguita Rarámuri (Tarahumara). *International Journal of American Linguistics*, 87(2), 149–178.

Caballero, G., C. Juárez Chávez & M. Yuan. (2024). The representation of tone in San Juan Piñas Mixtec (Tò'ōn Ndá'ví): Phonological and orthographic implications. In G. de la Cruz Sanchez, R. W. Smith, L. Irizarry, T. Ni & H. Harley (eds.), *Proceedings of WCCFL 35*, pp. 294–302. Cascadilla Press: Somerville, MA.

Cahill, M. & Rice, R. (eds.). (2014). *Developing Orthographies for Unwritten Languages*. Dallas, TX: SIL International.

Campbell, E. W. (2020). Probing phonological structure in play language: Speaking backwards in Zenzontepec Chatino. *Phonological Data and Analysis*, 2(1), 1–21.

Carpenter, J., Guerin, A., Kaczmarek, M., Lawson, G., Lawson, K., Nathan, L. P. & Turin, M. (2021). Locally contingent and community-dependent: Tools and technologies for Indigenous language mobilization. In A. Link, A. Shelton & P. Spero, eds., *Indigenous Languages and the Promise of Archives*. Lincoln, NE: University of Nebraska Press and The American Philosophical Society, pp. 125–155.

Chaparro Gardea, R. I., Fuentes Holguín, S., Fuentes Loya, B., Fuentes Moreno, G., Fuentes Palma, G., León Ramírez, L. E., Caballero, G. & Carroll, L. (2019). Materials of the Choguita Rarámuri Language Project, SCL 2019-01, Survey of California and Other Indian Languages. Berkeley, CA: University of California, Berkeley. http://dx.doi.org/doi:10.7297/X2HH6H70.

Coetzee, A. W. (2009). Learning lexical indexation. *Phonology*, 26(1), 109–145.

Coleman, J. & Pierrehumbert, J. (1997). Stochastic phonological grammars and acceptability. arXiv preprint: cmp-lg/9707017.

Coto-Solano, R., Akevai Nicholas, S., Datta, S., Quint, V., Wills, P., Ngakuravaru Powell, E., Koka'ua, L., Tanveer, S. & Feldman, I. (2022). Development of automatic speech recognition for the documentation of Cook Islands Māori. In N. Calzolari, F. Béchet, P. Blache, K. Choukri, C. Cieri, T. Declerck, S. Goggi, H. Isahara, B. Maegaard, J. Mariani, H. Mazo, J. Odijk & S. Piperidis, eds, *Proceedings of the Thirteenth Language Resources and Evaluation Conference*, Marseille, France, pp. 3872–3882.

Cristofaro, S. (2006). The organization of reference grammars: A typologist user's point of view. In F. K. Ameka, A. Dench & N. Evans, eds., *Catching Language: The Standing Challenge of Grammar Writing*. Berlin: De Gruyter Mouton, pp. 137–170.

Cruz Cruz, E. (ed.). (2020). Theoretical reflections around the role of fieldwork in linguistics and linguistic anthropology: Contributions of Indigenous researchers from southern Mexico. Translation from Spanish of *Reflexiones teóricas en torno a la función del trabajo de campo en lingüística-antropológica: contribuciones de investigadores indígenas del sur de México*. Language Documentation & Conservation Special Publication 22. Honolulu, HI: University of Hawai'i

Cruz, E. & Woodbury, A. C. (2014). Finding a way into a family of tone languages: The story and methods of the Chatino Language Documentation Project. *Language Documentation & Conservation*, 8, 490–524.

Currie Hall, K. (2022). Corpora and phonological analysis. In B. E. Dresher & H. van der Hulst, eds., *The Oxford History of Phonology*. Oxford: Oxford University Press, pp. 619–638.

Currie Hall, K., Pine, A. & Schwan, M. D. (2018). Doing phonological corpus analysis in a fieldwork context. In L. Matthewson, E. Guntly, M. Huijsmans & M. Rochemont, eds., *Wa7 Xweysás i Nqwal'utteníha i Ucwalmícwa: He Loves the People's Languages: Essays in Honour of Henry Davis*. Vancouver: Pacific Northwest Languages and Literatures, pp. 615–630.

Czaykowska-Higgins, E. (2009). Research models, community engagement, and linguistic fieldwork: Reflections on working within Canadian Indigenous communities. *Language Documentation & Conservation*, 3(1), 15–50.

Czaykowska-Higgins, E. (2018). Reflections on ethics: Re-humanizing linguistics, building relationships across difference. In B. McDonnell, A. L. Berez-Kroeker & G. Holton, eds., *Reflections on Language Documentation 20 Years After Himmelmann 1998*. Language Documentation & Conservation Special Publication no. 15. Honolulu, HI: University of Hawai'i Press, pp. 110–121.

Daly, J. P. & Hyman, L. (2007). On the representation of tone in Peñoles Mixtec. *International Journal of American Linguistics*, 73(2), 165–207.

Davis, H., Gillon, C. & Matthewson, L. (2014). How to investigate linguistic diversity: Lessons from the Pacific Northwest. *Language*, 90(4), e180–e226.

Davis, J. E. & McKay-Cody, M. (2010). Signed languages of American Indian communities: Considerations for interpreting work and research. In R. Locker McKee & J. E. Davies, eds., *Interpreting in Multilingual, Multicultural Contexts*. Washington, DC: Gallaudet University Press, pp. 119–157.

Di Carlo, P., Ojong Diba, R. A. & Good, J. (2021). Towards a coherent methodology for the documentation of small-scale multilingualism: Dealing with speech data. *International Journal of Bilingualism*, 25(4), 860–877.

Dingemanse, M. (2012). Advances in the cross-linguistic study of ideophones. *Language and Linguistics Compass*, 6(10), 654–672.

Dingemanse, M. (2018). Redrawing the margins of language: Lessons from research on ideophones. *Glossa: A Journal of General Linguistics*, 3(1), 4.

Döhler, C. (2018). *A Grammar of Komnzo*. Berlin: Language Science Press.

Duarte Borquez, C. (2023). Tone, prosodic structure and grammatical structure in San Juan Piñas Mixtec *(Tò'ōn Ndá'ví)*. Qualifying paper, UC San Diego.

Duarte Borquez, C., Juárez Chávez, C. & Caballero, G. (in press). Tonal upstep and downstep in San Juan Piñas Mixtec (Tò'ōn Ndá'ví). In D. K. E. Reisinger, ed., *Proceedings of WSCLA 26*, Vancouver: UBC Working Papers in Linguistics.

Elordieta, G. (2008). An overview of theories of the syntax–phonology interface. *Journal of Basque Linguistics and Philology*, 42, 209–286.

Epps, P. L., Webster, A. K. & Woodbury, A. C. (2023). Documenting speech play and verbal art: A tutorial. *Language Documentation and Conservation*, 26, 175–242.

Evans, N. (2012). Anything can happen: The verb lexicon and interdisciplinary fieldwork. In N. Thieberger, ed., *The Oxford Handbook of Linguistic Fieldwork*. Oxford: Oxford University Press, pp. 183–208.

Evans, N. & Dench, A. (2006). Introduction: Catching language. In F. K. Ameka, A. Dench & N. Evans, eds., *Catching Language: The Standing Challenge of Grammar Writing*. Berlin: De Gruyter Mouton, pp. 1–40.

Farris-Trimble, A. W. (2008). Cumulative faithfulness effects in phonology. PhD dissertation, Indiana University.

Fenlon, J. & Hochgesang, J. A., eds. (2022). *Signed Language Corpora*. Washington, DC: Gallaudet University Press.

Fischer, S. (2009). Sign language field methods: Approaches, techniques, and concerns. In J. H-Y Tai & J. Tsay, eds., *Taiwan Sign Language and Beyond*. Chia-Yi, Taiwan: The Taiwan Institute for the Humanities, National Chung Cheng University, pp. 1–19.

Fishman, J. (1977). *Advances in the Creation and Revision of Writing Systems*. The Hague: Mouton.

Fitzgerald, C. M. (1998). The meter of Tohono O'odham songs. *International Journal of American Linguistics*, 64(1), 1–36.

Fitzgerald, C. M. (2013). Revisiting Tohono O'odham high vowels. In S. T. Bischoff, D. Cole, A. V. Fountain & M. Miyashita, eds.,*The Persistence of Language: Constructing and Confronting the Past and Present in the Voices of Jane H. Hill*. Amsterdam: John Benjamins, pp. 107–132.

Fitzgerald, C. M. (2017). Motivating the documentation of the verbal arts: Arguments from theory and practice. *Language Documentation and Conservation*, 11, 114–132.

Flemming, E. (2001). Scalar and categorical phenomena in a unified model of phonetics and phonology. *Phonology*, 18, 7–44.

Frisch, S. A. & Zawaydeh, B. A. (2001). The psychological reality of OCP-Place in Arabic. *Language*, 77(1), 91–106.

Garellek, M., Aguilar, A., Caballero, G. & Carroll, L. (2015). Lexical and postlexical tone in Choguita Rarámuri. In M. Wolters, J. Livingstone, B. Beattie, R. Smith, M. MacMahon, J. Stuart-Smith & J. M. Scobbie, eds., *Proceedings of the 18th International Congress on Phonetic Sciences*. Glasgow, Scotland, August 10–14. Glasgow: University of Glasgow.

Garrett, A. (2023). *The Unnaming of Kroeber Hall: Language, Memory and Indigenous California*. Cambridge, MA: MIT Press.

Genetti, C. (2007). *A Grammar of Dolakha Newar*. Berlin: Mouton de Gruyter.

Gippert, J., N. P. Himmelmann & U. Mosel (eds.). (2006). *Essentials of Language Documentation*. Berlin: Mouton de Gruyter.

Goddard, P. E. (1904). *Hupa Texts*. University of California Publications in American Archaeology and Ethnology 1. Berkeley, CA: University of California.

Goldwater, S. & Johnson, M. (2003). Learning OT constraint rankings using a maximum entropy model. In J. Spenader, A. Eriksson & O. Dahl, eds., *Proceedings of the Stockholm Workshop on Variation within Optimality Theory*. Stockholm: Stockholm University, pp. 111–120.

Good, J. (2018). Ethics in language documentation and revitalization. In K. L. Rehg & L. Campbell, eds., *The Oxford Handbook of Endangered Languages*. Oxford: Oxford University Press, pp. 419–440.

Good, J. (2023). Adapting methods of language documentation to multilingual settings. *Journal of Language Contact*, 15(2), 341–375.

Gordon, M. K. (2016). *Phonological Typology*. Oxford: Oxford University Press.

Gouskova, M. (2018). Morphology and phonotactics. *Oxford Research Encyclopedia of Linguistics, Interactive Factory*. http://doi.org/10/1093/acrefore/9780199384655.013.

Grimm, N. (2021). *A grammar of Gyeli*. Berlin: Language Science Press.

Grimm, N. (2022). Documentary approaches to lexicography. In M. E. Ekpenyong & I. I. Udoh, eds., *Current Issues in Descriptive Linguistics and Digital Humanities: A Festschrift in Honor of Professor Eno-Abasi Essien Urua*. Singapore: Springer Nature Singapore, pp. 551–567.

Grinevald, C. (2003). Speakers and documentation of endangered languages. In P. K. Austin, ed., *Language Documentation and Description* (vol. 1). London: SOAS, pp. 52–72.

Guion, S. G., Amith, J. D., Doty, C. S. & Shport, I. A. (2010). Word-level prosody in Balsas Nahuatl: The origin, development, and acoustic correlates of tone in a stress accent language. *Journal of Phonetics*, 38(2), 137–166.

Gussenhoven, C. (2004). *The Phonology of Tone and Intonation*. Cambridge, UK: Cambridge University Press.

Hale, K., Krauss, M., Watahomigie, L. J., Yamamoto, A. Y., Craig, C., Masayesva, J. & England, N. (1992). Endangered languages. *Language*, 68, 1–42.

Halle, M. & Keyser, S. J. (1966). Chaucer and the study of prosody. *College English*, 28(3), 187–219.

Halle, M. & Keyser, S. J. (1971). Illustration and defense of a theory of the iambic pentameter. *College English*, 33(2), 154–176.

Harrington, J. P. (1932). *Tobacco Among the Karuk Indians of California*. Bureau of American Ethnology, Bulletin 94. Washington, DC: Government Printing Office.

Harrison, K. D., Lillehaugen, B. D. & Lopez, F. H. (2019). Zapotec language activism and Talking Dictionaries. In I. Kosem, T. Z. Kuhn, M. Correia, J. P. Ferreira, M. Jansen, I. Pereira, J. Kallas, M. Jakubíček, S. Krek & C. Tiberius, eds., *Electronic Lexicography in the 21st Century: Smart Lexicography: Proceedings of the eLex 2019 Conference*, pp. 31–50.

Hartmann, R. R. K. (1986). *The History of Lexicography*. Amsterdam: John Benjamins.

Haude, K. (2006). A grammar of Movima. PhD dissertation, Radboud University of Nijmegen.

Haviland, J. B. (2006). Documenting lexical knowledge. In J. Gippert, N. Himmelmann & U. Mosel, eds., *Essentials of Language Documentation*. Berlin: Mouton de Gruyter, pp. 129–162.

Hayes, B. (1989). The prosodic hierarchy in meter. In P. Kiparsky & G. Youmans, eds., *Rhythm and Meter, Volume 1: Phonetics and Phonology*. San Diego, CA: Academic Press, pp. 201–260.

Hayes, B. & Cziráky Londe, Z. (2006). Stochastic phonological knowledge: The case of Hungarian vowel harmony. *Phonology*, 23(1), 59–104.

Hayes, B. & Wilson, C. (2008). A maximum entropy model of phonotactics and phonotactic learning. *Linguistic Inquiry*, 39, 379–440.

Hayes, B. & Schuh, R. G. (2019). Metrical structure and sung rhythm of the Hausa rajaz. *Language*, 95(2), e253–e299.

Hayes, B., Wilson, C. & Shisko, A. (2012). Maxent grammars for the metrics of Shakespeare and Milton. *Language*, 88(4), 691–731.

Herrera Zendejas, E. (2014). *Formas sonoras: mapa fónico de las lenguas mexicanas*. México, D.F.: El Colegio de México.

Hildebrandt, K. A., Jany, C. & Silva, W. (2017). Introduction: Documenting variation in endangered languages. In K. A. Hildebrandt, C. Jany & W. Silva, eds., *Language Documentation & Conservation Special Publication No. 13: Documenting Variation in Endangered Languages*. University of Hawai'i Press, pp. 1–5. http://nlfrc.hawaii.edu/ldc/.

Hill, J. (2006a). The ethnography of language and language documentation. In J. Gippert, N. Himmelmann & U. Mosel, eds., *Essentials of Language Documentation*. Berlin: Mouton de Gruyter, pp. 113–128.

Hill, J. (2006b). Writing culture in grammar in the Americanist tradition. In F. K. Ameka, A. Dench & N. Evans, eds., *Catching Language: The Standing Challenge of Grammar Writing*. Berlin: Mouton de Gruyter, pp. 609–628.

Hill, J. H. & Nolasquez, R. (1973). *Mulu'wetam, the First People: Cupeño Oral History and Language*. Banning, CA: Malki Museum Press.

Himmelmann, N. (1998). Documentary and descriptive linguistics. *Linguistics*, 36, 161–195.

Himmelmann, N. (2006). Language documentation: What is it and what is it good for? In J. Gippert, N. Himmelmann & U. Mosel, eds., *Essentials of Language Documentation*. Berlin: Mouton de Gruyter, pp. 1–30.

Hinton, L. (2014). Orthography wars. In M. Cahill & K. Rice, eds., *Developing Orthographies for Unwritten Languages*. Dallas, TX: SIL International, pp. 139–168.

Hochgesang, J. A. (2019). Sign language description: A deaf retrospective and application of best practices from language documentation [Opening keynote presentation]. The 8th Meeting of Signed and Spoken Language Linguistics, National Museum of Ethnology, Minpaku, Osaka, Japan.

Hockett, C. F. (1966). The quantification of functional load: A linguistic problem. Report Number RM-5168-PR. Santa Monica: Rand Corp.

Holton, G. (2009). Relatively ethical: A comparison of linguistic research paradigms in Alaska and Indonesia. *Language Documentation & Conservation*, 3(2), 161–175.

Holton, G. (2018). Interdisciplinary language documentation. In K. Rehg & L. Campbell, eds., *Oxford Handbook of Endangered Languages*. Oxford: Oxford University Press, pp. 739–760.

Holton, G., Leonard, W. Y. & Pulsifer, P. L. (2022). Indigenous peoples, ethics, and linguistic data. In A. L. Berez-Kroeker, B. McDonnell, E. Koller & L. B. Collister, eds., *The Open Handbook of Linguistic Data Management*. Cambridge, MA: MIT Press, pp. 49–60.

Hou, L. L. Y-S. (2017). Negotiating language practices and language ideologies in fieldwork : A reflexive meta-documentation. In A. Kusters, M. de Meulder & D. O'Brien, eds., *Innovations in Deaf Studies: The Role of Deaf Scholars*. Oxford: Oxford University Press, pp. 339–359.

Hou, L. (2018). Iconic patterns in San Juan Quiahije Chatino Sign Language. *Sign Language Studies*, 18(4), 570–611.

Hou, L. & Kusters, A. (2020). Linguistic ethnography of signed languages. In K. Tusting, ed., *The Routledge Handbook of Linguistic Ethnography*. London: Routledge, pp. 340–355.

Hou, L. & de Vos, C. (2022). Classifications and typologies: Labeling sign languages and signing communities. *Journal of Sociolinguistics*, 26(1), 118–125.

Huaute, R. I. (2020). Expanding the documentation and description of conversational Cahuilla. Endangered Languages Archive. http://hdl.handle.net/2196/80d1c08f-52d7-464f-b243-0460edf84e38.

Huaute, R. I. (2022). A preliminary intonation model of Torres-Martinez Desert Cahuilla. In S. Frota, M. Cruz & M. Vigári, eds., *Proceedings of Speech Prosody*, May 23–26, 2022, Lisbon, Portugal. Lisbon: University of Lisbon, pp. 254–258.

Huaute, R. I. (2023). Topics in the phonology and morphology of Torres Martinez Desert Cahuilla. PhD dissertation, UC San Diego.

Huff, T. & Lapierre, M. (2021). The typologically rare approximant inventory of Kajkwakhrattxi: A series of natural sound changes. *Proceedings of the Linguistic Society of America*, 6(1), 855–868.

Hyman, L. M. (2011). Tone: Is it different? In J. Goldsmith, J. Riggle & A. Yu, ed., *The Handbook of Phonological Theory*, 2nd edn. London: Blackwell, pp. 197–239.

Hyman, L. M. (2018). Why underlying representations? *Journal of Linguistics*, 54(3), 591–610.

Hymes, D. (1971). The contribution of folklore to sociolinguistic research. *The Journal of American Folklore*, 84(331), 42–50.

Inkelas, S. (1997). The theoretical status of morphologically conditioned phonology: A case study of dominance effects. In G. Booij & J. van Marle, eds., *Yearbook of Morphology 1997*. Dordrecht: Springer Netherlands, pp. 121–155.

Inkelas, S. (2014). *The Interplay of Morphology and Phonology* (vol. 8). Oxford: Oxford University Press.

Itô, J. & Mester, A. (2003). *Japanese Morphophonemics: Markedness and Word Structure*. Linguistic Inquiry Monograph Series 41. Cambridge, MA: MIT Press.

Juárez Chávez, C., Caballero, G., Duarte Borquez, C., Fernández Guerrero, J. A., Huaute, R., Iyer, A., Tedeschi, N., Van Doren, M. & Yuan, M. (2022). *an Juan Piñas Mixtec (Tò'ōn Ndā'ví) Talking Dictionary*. Swarthmore College. www.talkingdictionary.org/sanjuanpinas.

Juárez Chávez, C., Pérez Morelos, B., Pérez Morelos, C., Caballero, G., Duarte Borquez, C., Kameda, T. & Yuan, M. (in press). Materials of the San Juan Piñas Mixtec Language Project. Survey of California and Other Indian Languages, University of California, Berkeley.

Jun, S. A. & Fletcher, J. (2014). Methodology of studying intonation: From data collection to data analysis. In S.-A. Jun, ed., *Prosodic Typology II: The Phonology of Intonation and Phrasing*. Oxford: Oxford University Press, pp. 493–519.

Katz, J. (2010). Compression effects, perceptual asymmetries, and the grammar of timing. PhD dissertation, Massachusetts Institute of Technology.

Katz, J. (2015). Hip-hop rhymes reiterate phonological typology. *Lingua*, 160, 54–74.

Kawahara, S. (2020). Sound symbolism and theoretical phonology. *Language and Linguistics Compass*, 14(8), e12372.

Kawahara, S., Katsuda, H. & Kumagai, G. (2019). Accounting for the stochastic nature of sound symbolism using Maximum Entropy model. *Open Linguistics*, 5(1), 109–120.

Kern, G. (2015). Rhyming grammars and Celtic phonology. PhD dissertation, Massachusetts Institute of Technology.

Kiparsky, P. (1975). Stress, syntax, and meter. *Language*, 51, 576–616.

Kiparsky, P. (1977). The rhythmic structure of English verse. *Linguistic Inquiry*, 8(2), 189–247.

Kiparsky, P. (1985). Some consequences of lexical phonology. *Phonology*, 2, 85–138.

Kirby, J. & Ladd, D. R. (2016). Tone–melody correspondence in Vietnamese popular song. Edinburgh: University of Edinburgh, ms.

Knoop, C. A., Blohm, S., Kraxenberger, M. & Menninghaus, W. (2021). How perfect are imperfect rhymes? Effects of phonological similarity and verse context on rhyme perception. *Psychology of Aesthetics, Creativity, and the Arts*, 15(3), 560–572.

Krämer, M. (2018). *Underlying Representations*. Cambridge, UK: Cambridge University Press.

Kramer, R. (2010). The Amharic definite marker and the syntax–morphology interface. *Syntax*, 13(3), 196–240.

Kresge, L. (2007). *Indigenous Oaxacan Communities in California: An Overview*. Davis, CA: California Institute for Rural Studies.

Kroeber, A. L. (1900). Cheyenne tales. *Journal of American Folklore*, 13, 161–190.

Kuang, J. & Cui, A. (2018). Relative cue weighting in production and perception of an ongoing sound change in Southern Yi. *Journal of Phonetics*, 71, 194–214.

Kusters, A. & Hou, L. (2020). Linguistic ethnography and sign language studies. *Sign Language Studies*, 20(4), 561–571.

Ladd, D. R. (2008). Intonational phonology. Cambridge, UK: Cambridge University Press.

Lapierre, M. (2023a). The phonology of Panãra: A segmental analysis. *International Journal of American Linguistics*, 89(2), 183–218.

Lapierre, M. (2023b). The phonology of Panãra: A prosodic analysis. *International Journal of American Linguistics*, 89(3), 333–356.

Lapierre, M. (2023c). Two types of [NT] s in Panãra: Evidence for temporally ordered subsegmental units. *Glossa: A Journal of General Linguistics*, 8(1).

Laycock, D. (1972). Towards a typology of ludlings, or play languages. *Linguistic Communications*, 6, 61–113.

Lee, A. P. (2017). Ideophones, interjections, and sound symbolism in Seediq. *Oceanic Linguistics*, 56(1), 181–209. http://www.jstor.org/stable/26408528.

Lefkowitz, M. (2017). Maxent Harmonic Grammars and phonetic duration. PhD dissertation, UCLA.

Leonard, W. Y. (2018). Reflections on (de) colonialism in language documentation. In B. McDonnell, A. L. Berez-Kroeker & G. Holton, eds., *Reflections on Language Documentation 20 Years after Himmelmann 1998*. Language Documentation & Conservation Special Publication No. 15, pp. 55–65.

Lin, I. (2019) Functional load, perception, and the learning of phonological alternations. PhD dissertation, University of California, Los Angeles.

Lindblom, B. (1986). Phonetic universals in vowel systems. In J. Ohala & J. Jaeger, eds., *Experimental Phonology*. Orlando, FL: Academic Press, pp. 13–44.

Łubowicz, A. (2005). Locality of conjunction. In J. Alderete, C. Han & A. Kochetov, eds., *Proceedings of the 24th West Coast Conference on Formal Linguistic*. Somerville: Cascadilla Press, pp. 254–262.

Marsaja, I. G. (2008). *Desa Kolok: A Deaf Village and Its Sign Language in Bali, Indonesia*. Nijmegen: Ishara Press.

Martin, J. B. (2011). *A Grammar of Creek (Muskogee)*. Lincoln, NE: University of Nebraska Press.

Martinet, A. (1952). Function, structure, and sound change. *Word*, 8(1), 1–32.

Mathiot, M. (1973). *A Dictionary of Papago Usage*. Bloomington, IN: Indiana University.

McKay-Cody, M. R. (1996). *Plains Indian Sign Language: A Comparative Study of Alternate and Primary Signers*. Masters thesis, University of Arizona.

McPherson, L. (2017a). Multiple feature affixation in Seenku plural formation. *Morphology*, 27, 217–252.

McPherson, L. (2017b). Tone features revisited: Evidence from Seenku. In J. Kandybowicz & H. Torrence, eds., *Diversity in African languages*. Oxford: Oxford University Press, pp. 297–320.

McPherson, L. (2018a). *Documenting Seenku (Mande, Burkina Faso) Language and Music, with Special Attention to Tone*. Endangered Languages Archive. http://hdl.handle.net/2196/00-0000-0000-0010-7D06-3.

McPherson, L. (2018b). The talking Balafon of the Sambla. *Anthropological Linguistics*, 60(3), 255–294.

McPherson, L. (2019a). Seenku argument-head tone sandhi: Allomorph selection in a cyclic grammar. *Glossa: A Journal of General Linguistics*, 4(1), 22.

McPherson, L. (2019b). Musical adaptation as phonological evidence: Case studies from textsetting, rhyme, and musical surrogates. *Language and Linguistics Compass*, 13(12), e12359.

McPherson, L. (2020). *A Grammar of Seenku* (vol. 83). Berlin: de Gruyter Mouton.

McPherson, L. (in press, a). A collaborative methodology for grammatical tone acquisition in Seenku. In V. Carstens, K. Russell, O. Akingbade, D. Morton & M. Diercks, eds., *Selected Papers from the 54th Annual Conference on African Linguistics*. Language Science Press.

McPherson, L. (in press, b). The acquisition of verbal tone in Seenku (Mande, Burkina Faso). *First Language*.

McPherson, L. & James, L. (2021). Artistic adaptation of Seenku tone: Musical surrogates vs. vocal music. In A. Akinlabi, L. Bickmore, M. Cahill, M. Diercks, L. J. Downing, J. Essegbey, K. Franich, L. McPherson & S. Rose, eds., *Celebrating 50 Years of ACAL: Selected Papers from the 50th Annual Conference on African Linguistics* (Contemporary African Linguistics 7). Berlin: Language Science Press, pp. 203–223.

McPherson, L. & Ryan, K. M. (2018). Tone–tune association in Tommo So (Dogon) folk songs. *Language*, 94(1), 119–156.

McPherson, L. & Winter, Y. (2022). Surrogate languages and the grammar of language-based music. *Frontiers in Communication*, 7, 838286.

Michael, L. (2019). Lines in Nanti karintaa chants: An areal poetic typological perspective (An essay in honor of Joel Sherzer). *Cadernos de Etnolingüística: Estudos de Lingüística Sul-Americana*, 7(1), 56–64.

Miyashita, M. (2011). Five Blackfoot lullabies. *Proceedings of the American Philosophical Society*, 155(3), 276–293.

Mohanan, K. P. (1982). Lexical phonology. PhD dissertation, Massachusetts Institute of Technology.

Morgan, H. E. (2022). *A Phonological Grammar of Kenyan Sign Language* (vol. 11). Berlin: Walter de Gruyter.

Mosel, U. (2006). Grammaticography: The art and craft of writing grammars. In F. K. Ameka, A. Dench & N. Evans, eds., *Catching Language: The Standing Challenge of Grammar Writing*. Berlin: Mouton de Gruyter, pp. 41–68.

Mosel, U. (2011). Lexicography in endangered language communities. In P. Austin & J. Sallabank, eds., *The Cambridge Handbook of Endangered Languages*. Cambridge, UK: Cambridge University Press, pp. 337–353.

Mosel, U. (2014). Corpus linguistic and documentary approaches in writing a grammar of a previously undescribed language. In T. Nakayama & K. Rice, eds., *Language Documentation & Conservation Special Publication No. 8: The Art and Practice of Grammar Writing*. Honolulu, HI: University of Hawai'i Press, pp. 135–157.

Mosel, U. (2018). Corpus compilation and exploitation in language documentation projects. In K. L. Rehg & L. Campbell, eds., *The Oxford Handbook of Endangered Languages*. Oxford: Oxford University Press, pp. 248–270.

Nakayama, T. & Rice, K. (eds.). (2014). *The Art and Practice of Grammar Writing*. Language Documentation and Conservation Special Publication No. 8. Hawai'i: University of Hawai'i Press.

Nelson, N. R. & Wedel, A. (2017). The phonetic specificity of competition: Contrastive hyperarticulation of voice onset time in conversational English. *Journal of Phonetics*, 64, 51–70.

Newell, H. (2018). The syntax–phonology interface in Rule-Based Phonology. In S. J. Hannahs & A. R. K. Bosch, eds., *The Routledge Handbook of Phonological Theory*. London: Routledge, pp. 197–225.

Nigmatulina, I., Kew, T. & Samardzic, T. (2020). ASR for non-standardised languages with dialectal variation: The case of Swiss German. In M. Zampieri, P. Nakov, N. Ljubešić, J. Tiedemann & Y Scherrer, eds., *Proceedings of the 7th Workshop on NLP for Similar Languages, Varieties and Dialects*. International Committee on Computational Linguistics (ICCL), pp. 15–24.

Norris, M. (2014). A theory of nominal concord. PhD dissertation, UC Santa Cruz.

Nyst, V. (2007). A descriptive analysis of Adamorobe sign language (Ghana). PhD dissertation, University of Amsterdam.

Nyst, V. (2015). Sign language fieldwork. In E. Orfanidou, B. Woll & G. Morgan, eds., *Research Methods in Sign Language Studies: A Practical Guide*. Chichester: Wiley-Blackwell, pp. 107–122.

Nyst, V. (2019). The impact of cross-linguistic variation in gesture on sign language phonology and morphology: The case of size and shape specifiers. *Gesture*, 18(2–3), 343–369.

Nyst, V. A. S., Baker, A. E., Bogaerde, B. & Crasborn, O. A. (2003). The phonology of name signs: A comparison between the sign languages of Uganda, Mali, Adamorobe and the Netherlands. In A. Baker, B. van den Bogaerde & O. Alex Crasborn, eds., *Cross-Linguistic Perspectives in Sign Language Research. Selected Papers from TISLR 2000.* Washington, DC: Gallaudet University Press, pp. 71–80.

Odden, D. A. & Bickmore, L. (2014). Melodic tone in Bantu: Overview. *Africana Linguistica*, 20(1), 3–13.

Oh, Y. M., Coupé, C., Marsico, E. & Pellegrino, F. (2015). Bridging phonological system and lexicon: Insights from a corpus study of functional load. *Journal of Phonetics*, 53, 153–176.

Padden, C. (2015). Methods of research on sign language grammars. In E. Orfanidou, B. Woll & G. Morgan, eds., *Research Methods in Sign Language Studies: A Practical Guide.* Chichester: Wiley-Blackwell, pp. 141–155.

Palancar, E. L. (2016). A typology of tone and inflection: A view from the Oto-Manguean languages of Mexico. In E. L. Palancar & J.-L. Léonard, eds., *Tone and Inflection: New Facts and New Perspectives.* Berlin: Walter De Gruyter, pp. 109–139.

Palancar, E. L., Amith, J. D. & Castillo García, R. (2016). Verbal inflection in Yoloxóchitl Mixtec. In E. L. Palancar & J.-L. Léonard, eds., *Tone and Inflection: New Facts and New Perspectives.* Berlin: Walter De Gruyter, pp. 295–336.

Pater, J. (2010). Morpheme-specific phonology: Constraint indexation and inconsistency resolution. In S. Parker, ed., *Phonological Argumentation: Essays on Evidence and Motivation.* Toronto: University of Toronto Press, pp. 123–154.

Pater, J. (2016). Universal Grammar with weighted constraints. In J. J. McCarthy & J. Pater, eds., *Harmonic Grammar and Harmonic Serialism.* London: Equinox, pp. 1–46.

Payne, T. E. & Weber, D. J. (eds.). (2007). *Perspectives on Grammar Writing.* Amsterdam: John Benjamins.

Peust, C. (2014). Towards a typology of poetic rhyme. In E. Grossman, M. Haspelmath, T. S. Richter, eds., *EgyptianCoptic Linguistics in Typological Perspective* (Empirical Approaches to Language Typology [EALT] 55), Berlin: de Gruyter Mouton, pp. 341–385.

Pierrehumbert, J. & Beckman, M. (1988). *Japanese Tone Structure.* Cambridge, MA: MIT Press.

Pike, E. V. & Wistrand, K. (1974). Step-up terrace tone in Acatlán Mixtec. In R. Brend, ed., *Advances in Tagmemics*. Amsterdam: North-Holland Publishing Company, pp. 83–104.

Poser, W. J. (1984). The phonetics and phonology of tone and intonation in Japanese. PhD dissertation, Massachusetts Institute of Technology.

Potts, C., Pater, J., Jesney, K., Bhatt, R. & Becker, M. (2010). Harmonic Grammar with linear programming: From linear systems to linguistic typology. *Phonology*, 27, 77–117.

Prud'hommeaux, E., Jimerson, R., Hatcher, R. & Michelson, K. (2021). Automatic speech recognition for supporting endangered language documentation. *Language Documentation & Conservation*, 15, 491–513.

Pye, C., Ingram, D. & List, H. (1987). A comparison of initial consonant acquisition in English and Quiché. In K. Nelson & A. Van Kleek, eds., *Children's Language* (vol. 6). Hillsdale, MI: Erlbaum, pp. 175–190.

Rainie, S. C., Kukutai, T., Walter, M., Figueroa-Rodríguez, O. L., Walker, J. & Axelsson, P. (2019). Issues in open data: Indigenous data sovereignty. In T. Davies, S. B. Walker, M. Rubinstein & F. Perini, eds., *State of Open Data*. Cape Town: African Minds, pp. 300–319. https://doi.org/10.5281/zenodo.2677801.

Rarrick, S. & Wilson, B. (2016). Documenting Hawai'i's sign languages. *Language Documentation & Conservation*, 10, 337–346.

Remijsen, B. & Ayoker, O. G. (2021). The noun phrase in Shilluk. In *Language Documentation & Conservation Special Publication No. 14: A Grammar of Shilluk*. Manoa, HI: University of Hawai'i Press, pp. 1–91.

Rice, K. (2010). The linguist's responsibilities to the community of speakers: Community-based research. In L. A. Grenoble & N. Louanna Furbee, eds., *Language Documentation: Practice and Values*. Amsterdam: John Benjamins, pp. 25–36.

Rice, K. (2011a). Ethics in fieldwork. In N. Thieberger, ed., *The Oxford Handbook of Linguistic Fieldwork*. Oxford: Oxford University Press, pp. 407–429.

Rice, K. (2011b). Documentary linguistics and community relations. *Language Documentation & Conservation*, 5, 187–207.

Rice, K. (2018). Reflections on documenting the lexicon. In B. McDonnell, A. L. Berez-Kroeker & G. Holton, eds., *Language Documentation & Conservation Special Publication No. 15: Reflections on Language Documentation 20 Years After Himmelmann 1998*. Manoa, HI: University of Hawai'i Press, pp. 183–190.

Rice, R. (2014). Sounds in grammar writing. In T. Nakayama & K. Rice, eds., *Language Documentation & Conservation Special Issue: The Art and*

Practice of Grammar Writing. Manoa, HI: University of Hawai'i Press, pp. 69–89.

Rueda Chaves, J. E. (2019). La interacción entre el tono y el acento en el mixteco de San Jerónimo de Xayacatlán. PhD dissertation, El Colegio de México.

Ryan, K. M. (2011). Gradient syllable weight and weight universals in quantitative metrics. *Phonology*, 28(3), 413–454.

Ryan, K. M. (2014). Onsets contribute to syllable weight: Statistical evidence from stress and meter. *Language*, 90(2), 309–341.

Sande, H. (2019). Phonologically determined nominal concord as postsyntactic: Evidence from Guébie. *Journal of Linguistics*, 55(4), 831–878.

Sapir, E. (1910). *Yana Texts*. University of California Publications in American Archaeology and Ethnology 9. Berkeley, CA: University of California Press.

Sapir, E. (1912). The Takelma language of southwestern Oregon. *Handbook of American Indian Language*, Bulletin 40. Bureau of American Ethnology. Washington, DC: Smithsonian Institution, pp. 1–296.

Sapir, E. (1921). *Language: An Introduction to the Study of Speech*. New York: Harcourt, Brace and Company.

Sauvel, K. S. & Munro, P. (1981). 'Chem'ivillu' (Let's Speak Cahuilla). Los Angeles, CA: American Indian Studies Center, University of California, Los Angeles.

Schellenberg, M. (2012). Does language determine music in tone languages?. *Ethnomusicology*, 56(2), 266–278.

Schmaling, C. (2000). *Maganar Hannu, Language of the Hands: A Descriptive Analysis of Hausa Sign Language*. Hamburg: Signum.

Sebba, M. (2007). *Spelling and Society: The Culture and Politics of Orthography Around the World*. Cambridge, UK: Cambridge University Press.

Seidl, A. (2013). *Minimal Indirect Reference: A Theory of the Syntax–Phonology Interface*. New York: Routledge.

Seifart, F., Evans, N., Hammarström, H. & Levinson, S. C. (2018). Language documentation twenty-five years on. *Language*, 94(4), e324–e345.

Seiler, H. (1965). Accent and morphophonemics in Cahuilla and in Uto-Aztecan. *International Journal of American Linguistics*, 31(1), 50–59.

Seiler, H. (1970). Cahuilla texts with an introduction (vol. 6). Bloomington, IN: Indiana University.

Seiler, H. (1977). Cahuilla grammar. Banning, CA: Malki Museum Press.

Seiler, H. & Hioki, K. (1979). *Cahuilla Dictionary*. Banning, CA: Malki Museum Press.

Selkirk, E. (2011). The syntax–phonology interface. In J. Goldsmith, J. Riggle & A. C. L. Yu, eds., *The Handbook of Phonological Theory*. Hoboken, NJ: Blackwell, pp. 435–484.

Sherzer, J. (2002). *Speech Play and Verbal Art*. Austin, TX: University of Texas Press.

Shih, S. (2017). Constraint conjunction in weighted probabilistic grammar. *Phonology*, 34(2), 243–268.

Si, A. (2011). Biology in language documentation. *Language Documentation and Conservation*, 5, 169–186.

Skilton, A. (2017). Three speakers, four dialects: Documenting variation in an endangered Amazonian language. In K. A. Hildebrandt, C. Jany & W. Silva, eds., *Language Documentation & Conservation Special Publication No. 13: Documenting Variation in Endangered Languages*. Manoa, HI: University of Hawai'i Press, pp. 94–115.

Sleeper, M. & Reyes Basurto, G. (2022). Musicolinguistic documentation: Tone & tune in Tlahuapa Tù'un Sàví songs. *Language Documentation & Conservation*, 16, 168–208.

Smith, J. L. (2011). Category-specific effects. In M. van Oostendorp, C. Ewen, E. Hume & K. Rice, eds., *The Blackwell Companion to Phonology* (vol. 4). Hoboken, NJ: Wiley-Blackwell, pp. 2439–2463.

Smolensky, P. (2006). Optimality in phonology II: Harmonic completeness, local constraint conjunction, and feature domain markedness. In P. Smolensky & G. Legendre, eds., *The Harmonic Mind: From Neural Computation to Optimality-Theoretic Grammar. Volume 2: Linguistic and Philosophical Implications*. Cambridge, MA: MIT Press, pp. 27–160.

Snider, K. L. (1988) Towards the representation of tone: A three dimensional approach. In H. van der Hulst & N. Smith, eds., *Features, Segmental Structure and Harmony Processes* (vol. 1). Dordrecht: Foris Publications, pp. 237–269.

Snider, K. (2014). Orthography and phonological depth. In M. Cahill & K. Rice, eds., *Developing Orthographies for Unwritten Languages*. Dallas, TX: SIL International Publications in Language Use and Education, pp. 27–48.

Snider, K. L. (2018). *Tone Analysis for Field Linguists*. Dallas, TX: SIL International Publications.

Stanford, J. N. & Preston, D. R. (eds.). (2009). *Variation in Indigenous Minority Languages*. Amsterdam: John Benjamins.

Truckenbrodt, H. (2007). The syntax–phonology interface. In P. de Lacy, ed., *The Cambridge Handbook of Phonology*. Cambridge, UK: Cambridge University Press, pp. 435–456.

van den Berg, R. (2024). Lexicography and language documentation: Urgency, challenges, possibilities. *Lexicography*. https://doi.org/10.1558/lexi.27796.

van Severen, L., Gillis, J. J., Molemans, I., Van Den Berg, R., De Maeyer, S. & Gillis, S. (2012). The relation between order of acquisition, segmental frequency and function: The case of word-initial consonants in Dutch. *Journal of Child Language*, 40(4), 703–740.

Visser, E. (2022). *A Grammar of Kalamang*. Berlin: Language Science Press.

Voegelin, C. F. (1935). Tübatalabal texts. *University of California Publication in American Archaeology and Ethnology*, 34, 191–246.

Walshaw, C. (2011). The abc music standard 2.1. http://abcnotation.com/wiki/abc:standard:v2.1 (accessed May 20, 2018).

Wassink, A. B., Gansen, C. & Bartholomew, I. (2022). Uneven success: Automatic speech recognition and ethnicity-related dialects. *Speech Communication*, 140, 50–70.

Wedel, A., Kaplan, A. & Jackson, S. (2013). High functional load inhibits phonological contrast loss: A corpus study. *Cognition*, 128(2), 179–186.

Weeda, D. S. (1992). Word truncation in prosodic morphology. PhD dissertation, The University of Texas at Austin.

Whalen, D. H. & McDonough, J. (2019). Under-researched languages: Phonetic results from language archives. In W. F. Katz & P. F. Assman, eds., *The Routledge Handbook of Phonetics*. London: Routledge, pp. 51–71.

Wong, P. C. M. & Diehl, R. D. (2002). How can the lyrics of a song in a tone language be understood?. *Psychology of Music*, 30(2), 202–209.

Woodbury, A. (2003). Defining documentary linguistics. *Language Documentation and Description*, 1, 35–51.

Woodbury, A. (2011). Language documentation. In P. Austin & J. Sallabank, eds., *The Cambridge Handbook of Endangered Languages*. Cambridge, UK: Cambridge University Press, pp. 159–186.

Zeshan, U. 2000. *Sign Language in Indo-Pakistan: A Description of a Signed Language*. Philadelphia, PA: John Benjamins.

Zuraw, K. R. (2000). Patterned exceptions in phonology. PhD dissertation, University of California, Los Angeles.

Zymet, J. (2018). Lexical propensities in phonology: Corpus and experimental evidence, grammar, and learning. PhD dissertation, University of California, Los Angeles.

Phonology

Robert Kennedy
University of California, Santa Barbara

Robert Kennedy is a Senior Lecturer in Linguistics at the University of California, Santa Barbara. His research has focused on segmental and rhythmic alternations in reduplicative phonology, with an emphasis on interactions among stress patterns, morphological structure, and allomorphic phenomena, and socio-phonological variation within and across the vowel systems of varieties of English. His work has appeared in *Linguistic Inquiry, Phonology*, and *American Speech*. He is also the author of *Phonology: A Coursebook* (Cambridge University Press), an introductory textbook for students of phonology.

Patrycja Strycharczuk
University of Manchester

Patrycja Strycharczuk is a Senior Lecturer in Linguistics and Quantitative Methods at the University of Manchester. Her research programme is centered on exploring the sound structure of language by using instrumental articulatory data. Her major research projects to date have examined the relationship between phonology and phonetics in the context of laryngeal processes, the morphology-phonetics interactions, and articulatory dynamics as a factor in sound change. The results of these investigations have appeared in journals such as *Journal of Phonetics, Laboratory Phonology*, and *Journal of the Acoustical Society of America*. She has received funding from the British Academy and the Arts and Humanities Research Council.

Editorial Board
Diana Archangeli, *University of Arizona*
Ricardo Bermúdez-Otero, *University of Manchester*
Jennifer Cole, *Northwestern University*
Silke Hamann, *University of Amsterdam*

About the Series
Cambridge Elements in Phonology is an innovative series that presents the growth and trajectory of phonology and its advancements in theory and methods, through an exploration of a wide range of topics, including classical problems in phonology, typological and aerial phenomena, and interfaces and extensions of phonology to neighbouring disciplines.

Cambridge Elements

Phonology

Elements in the Series

Coarticulation in Phonology
Georgia Zellou

Complexity in the Phonology of Tone
Lian-Hee Wee and Mingxing Li

Quantitative and Computational Approaches to Phonology
Jane Chandlee

Psycholinguistics and Phonology: The Forgotten Foundations of Generative Phonology
Naiyan Du and Karthik Durvasula

Issues in Metrical Phonology: Insights from Ukrainian
Beata Łukaszewicz and Janina Mołczanow

Second Language Phonology: Phonetic Variation and Phonological Representations
Ellen Simon

Phonology in Language Documentation
Gabriela Caballero and Laura McPherson

A full series listing is available at: www.cambridge.org/EPHO

For EU product safety concerns, contact us at Calle de José Abascal, 56–1°,
28003 Madrid, Spain or eugpsr@cambridge.org.

www.ingramcontent.com/pod-product-compliance
Lightning Source LLC
LaVergne TN
LVHW011858060526
838200LV00054B/4398